IF I
ACCEPT
THE TRUTH

RICKY CLEMONS

PUBLISHED BY FIDELI PUBLISHING, INC.

ISBN: 978-1-955622-34-9

Published by

Fideli Publishing, Inc.
119 W. Morgan St.
Martinsville, IN 46151
www.FideliPublishing.com

Table of Contents

If I Accept the Truth

If I accept the truth of the bad things that I did in my life many years ago, then the Lord can spiritually heal me.

I must accept the truth about my past sins and confess and repent of those past sins unto the Lord.

If I accept the truth about my life, then the Lord can spiritually heal me to spiritually mature in His amazing grace.

If I don't accept the truth about the bad things that I did in my life, then I am still in bondage today.

Accepting my past life and being remorseful about it is the beginning of my journey for the Lord to heal me mentally, emotionally and spiritually.

The truth about my past life is all of my truth that I can't deny.

I can't pretend like I always had my life together.

I can't pretend like I've always been good.

If I accept the truth about my past life and own up to it, the Lord can heal me from lying to myself, who the Lord showed His great mercy on for me to accept my truth and tell my truth to set me free and hopefully someone else free from lying to oneself.

I am a new man in my Lord, Jesus Christ, today because I accepted Jesus Christ as my Lord and savior.

I have confessed and repented of my past old sins, and today I can't pretend like I have no sins.

The Lord commands us to love one another and we must tell one another the truth about ourselves for the Lord to spiritually heal us.

I must accept the truth about myself in order to tell the truth about myself to others, who must accept the truth about their past and present life for the Lord to spiritually heal them.

Accepting the truth about oneself is not always easy because it surely takes a great deal of maturing to accept the truth about oneself and tell your truth to others.

You and I are in the same boat and have to accept the truth about our past and present sins, whether we have many or few sins.

You and I must look deep within ourselves to see that Jesus Christ has paid our price on the cross to save us from our sins.

Jesus is so full of mercy and grace to allow you and me to use our truths to be a testimony about Him, while He gives us the strength to accept the truth about ourselves and our past sins.

If I live my life like I never had any past sins and Jesus never brought me through it, then I would be a liar and I'd just be playing Church.

Jesus is the only judge who will judge my past and present life that He gave to me with a free will to reap what I sow.

The blood of Jesus Christ has washed away all of my past sins that made me feeble-minded and do unacceptable things.

I thank the Lord today for helping me to accept the truth about my past sins that He cleansed from me so that I could be strong enough today to tell my truth to the world — that I haven't always been a Christian.

I truly love being a Christian today, and I accept the truth about the bad things that anyone can do, because we all are sinners saved by grace

When I accepted the truth about my past sins, it was like seeing the sun rising in the early morning.

Seeing the sunrise is a beautiful sight to see.

The beautiful sunrise lights up the dry land and the deep ocean waters that look so true to you and me.

There are no more ifs about me not accepting the truth about my past sins that the Lord has cleansed me from so that I am like the beautiful sun rising up in the sky that hovers over the truth about everyone's past and present life.

The Lord has forgiven me of my past sins, and the Lord helped me to forgive myself of my past sins when I accepted the truth.

Where sin abounds, grace abounds much more in my life for me to claim the promises God made to me.

Today I know that I belong to the Lord and I am not outside of God's mercy and grace.

I have accepted the truth about my past sins that the Lord washed away in His precious blood.

I am not without sin today, but I am a new spiritually true man and will not commit those past sins anymore.

I thank the Lord for making me very aware that I was not too lost in my past sins for Him to let the devil destroy me.

The Lord foreknew before I was born that I would accept the truth about everything in my life, but the Lord didn't overlook me and gave me a chance to confess and repent.

I am not completely free from sin today, but I am happy to know that the Lord accepted my truth and didn't condemn me in my past sins that have no control over me today because my Lord and Savior Jesus Christ cleanse me of my past sins.

I was Young and Foolish

I grew up without a father in the home.

During my high school years, I played a lot of hooky from going to school.

I would leave out of the house and pretend that I was going to school, but then I would hide behind the house until my mother went to work.

After my mother left out of the house, I would go back in the house and watch TV.

I would also bake buttered bread in the oven and cook some eggs on the stove.

I played hooky from school and don't even know why I did it.

When I did go to school, no one asked me where I had been.

I also don't remember my mother ever looking at my report cards to see my grade and my attendance in school.

I don't know how I was able to pass my classes in high school.

I passed from the ninth grade to the tenth grade and from the eleventh grade to the twelfth grade with a C grade point average.

If I had taken going to school seriously, I believe that my grades would have been much higher.

I was young and foolish, because when I did go to school I would hang around with bad company and drink wine after school was over.

I believed that I was having a good time, but I didn't see how foolish I was.

I deceived my mother when I made her believe that I was going to school, but most of all I deceived myself and robbed myself of the opportunity to do my best in school.

I was young and foolish, but there were many other young and wise high school students who graduated with a high grade point average and went on to college.

I feel regret today because I did not take going to school seriously, but the Lord showed mercy on me and allowed me to be doing as well as I am today.

I was young and foolish and didn't know it, but I know today that I am serious about living my life unto the Lord Jesus Christ.

The Lord has helped me to wise up so that I know that education is for life, especially getting educated about God's holy word that is full of wisdom to get the foolishness out of anyone.

For a Long Time

The devil has been trying to destroy me for a long time, because he knew that when I gave my life unto the Lord there would be no turning back to him.

The devil has tried to destroy me since I was a little child, like when I was sexually assaulted.

The devil tried to destroy me when I was a little boy who was trapped in the trunk of an old car. The devil tried to destroy me when I was a teenager who drank alcohol and smoked cigarettes.

The devil tried his best to destroy me.

The Lord didn't let the devil destroy me because the Lord knew that I would one day give my life unto Him.

The devil tried to destroy me in my young adult years when I used drugs that caused me to have a nervous breakdown that lasted the rest of my young adult years.

God knew that the devil didn't want me to live to see the day where I truly know that the Lord God, Jesus Christ brought me this far.

Jesus Christ has brought me this far so that I can love and obey Him day after day.

For a long time, the devil tried to destroy me because he knew that I would give my life to the Lord, and give my Lord Jesus Christ my best, regardless of what I went through in my life.

The devil tried to destroy me for a long time.

He tried to destroy me when a group of young men beat me up at a party that I wasn't invited to.

The devil tried to destroy me when a drunken man put a gun to my head.

The devil tried to destroy me when my manic depressive first wife put a knife to my throat while I was driving her to the naval hospital for a biopsy.

She died from breast cancer some months later because she refused to get chemotherapy treatments.

The Lord God Jesus Christ didn't let her kill me when she put that knife to my throat.

The devil tried to destroy me when I went to jail.

My manic depressive first wife was abusive towards me and I tried to defend myself and get away from her, but she followed behind me when I ran outside the apartment and I was arrested because some neighbor called the police.

The Lord didn't let the devil destroy me in jail where I was locked up for four months.

The devil tried to destroy me when I fell asleep while driving my car home from work.

The Lord woke me up in a matter of a few seconds, and I was shocked to see that I was right beside a tractor trailer truck that I could have swerved into.

God didn't let the devil destroy me because God knew that when I gave my life unto Him I would give testimonies about what He brought me through.

God has been with me for a long time, and the devil hates that because God didn't let him destroy me, which means I get to see this day that I know I truly don't deserve to be alive.

The devil tried to destroy me when I was having a sexual relationship with some married women.

I had a sexual relationship with one of the women in her husband's house, and the Lord showed mercy on me and didn't let her husband walk in on us.

The devil tried to destroy me when I got involved in a deadly quarrel between a man and a woman one night.

The man was very mad at his girlfriend and left the house.

He ran down the street and came back with a long metal pipe in his hand, which I saw when I left out of the house.

I looked to see where he went, and I saw him running very fast toward me with the long metal pipe in his hand as I held a long knife in my hand.

I know today that the Lord stopped him in his tracks to keep him from hitting me with that metal pipe, which could have killed me.

The devil tried to destroy me a long time ago, but the Lord spared my life even through all of my ignorance and mistakes that the devil used to try to destroy me.

There were other things that happened in my life that the devil used to try to destroy me too, but the Lord Almighty protected my life and kept me from death and the early grave that I deserved when the Lord knew that I would be a new creature in Him today.

The devil tried to destroy me a long time ago when I was an 18-year-old virgin who joined the military and then had sex with a prostitute.

The Lord showed mercy on me and didn't allow me to get a deadly venereal disease.

My Lord God and Savior Jesus Christ didn't let the devil destroy me in my rebellion against Him.

The devil tried to destroy me simply because I exist and have the opportunity to be saved in Jesus Christ and make it to heaven where the devil once lived but got kicked out of.

The devil tried to destroy me in my sins because he didn't want me to exist today to live for the Lord.

God gave the devil a chance to repent up in heaven, but the devil's chances had run out.

The Lord didn't let the devil destroy me in my sins, because the Lord knew that He could use me because He foresaw me confessing and repenting of my sins and denying myself and picking up my cross to follow Him.

The devil hated to see that happen because he knew that my soul would be anchored in the Lord and there would be no turning back to my past life that the devil had tried to destroy a long time ago when the Lord overthrew his attempts.

I know that there were many other people who are not here in the land of the living today and I don't know the reason why they didn't make it this far.

I know that I can't question God about that because God always knows what He is doing and what He must do for the good of everyone.

The devil tried to destroy everyone a long time ago, and God allowed him to succeed in destroying many people.

I know that I am no better than those people who the devil destroyed a long time ago.

I don't completely know why the Lord God Jesus Christ spared my life and let me see this day that many people had hoped to see.

The devil tried his best to destroy me a long time ago, but the Lord God Jesus Christ looked down on me from heaven and saw something in me that got His attention and He did not let the devil destroy me.

I believe that if I was the only sinner in a world of perfect people, the Lord would have given up His life for me to be saved and make it to Heaven.

God has given me the opportunity to know this today, and I realize He can give a long life to anyone who He chooses and no one can question Him about it.

The devil tried to destroy me a long time ago, and the devil made accusations against me that were true for me to not deserve to be here today, but the Lord confused the devil by lengthening my days so I could see this day of living my life unto the Him.

The devil tried to destroy me when I tried to take my own life by taking an overdose of sleeping pills.

The Lord used my girlfriend to save my life.

I woke up in the hospital the next day.

God didn't let the devil destroy me a long time ago when I was weak-minded and would fall for just about anything the devil tempted me with.

I am so glad today that the Lord didn't give up on me, even when I had given up on myself.

I am happy to give this testimony today about what the Lord brought me through when no one else could bring me through my failures and misfortunes.

God didn't let the devil get the victory over me, and my life was not cut short from the land of the living.

I was spiritually blind a long time ago, but thanks to the Lord, today I see that my soul was never worthless to God who did not let the devil destroy me a long time ago.

That long time ago is like a split second to God, but all it takes is a split second to die in a car accident.

To God, my past life flashed by like a car light flashing by a tree in the night.

God didn't let the devil destroy me a long time ago.

Even though my death might have flashed by many times, God spared my life even when I didn't deserve it.

The devil tried to destroy me a long time ago when I smoked marijuana, smoked hash, used LSD and smoked crack cocaine.

My God, Lord and Savior Jesus Christ didn't let the devil destroy me through those drugs.

I am so glad that the Lord is not finished with me so that I can give my testimonies about all the terrible things that He brought me through.

That old devil didn't want me to live to see this day where I can share with the world that God cannot fail to let you and me live a long life even though the devil sets many death traps for us.

A long time ago, God didn't let the devil destroy me in my sins, and since I gave my life to Him, the Lord has cleansed me from doing those bad things that I did a long time ago.

Today I am a new creature in my Lord and Savior Jesus Christ.

That old sinful me was gone the second I gave my life to Jesus Christ.

The devil tried to destroy me a long time ago, when I was an unarmed security officer who was picking up something at a convenience store.

While I was there, a black man approached me, got all up in my face to start a fight with me.

There were four other black men with him and one of them said, "Let's go," to the man who wanted to start a fight with me.

I know today that it was the Lord who protected me.

That man could have shot me with the gun if the other man hadn't said, "Let's go."

The Lord God didn't let the devil take my life a long time ago.

The devil tried to destroy me a long time ago when I was walking through a violent apartment complex one day and a young man and boy approached me.

They stopped me in my tracks and asked, "What's up, man?"

I said, "The Lord is my redeemer."

There was another man who laughed and said. "Homeboy's mind is gone."

So, the young black man and young boy moved away from me and let me go where I was going.

The Lord protected me that night a long time ago.

The Lord God didn't let the devil destroy me a long time ago.

It's a miracle to me to see this day where I can give my testimonies about what the Lord brought me through.

The devil tried to destroy me when I got circumcised at the age of 14 years old.

I was in so much pain for the whole summer months.

I couldn't do much of anything at all.

My mother had to comfort me when I felt like I would die from the terrible pain.

The Lord didn't let the devil destroy me a long time ago when I was a teenage boy.

The Lord has blessed me to be 64 years old today, and I can look back on my life and know that I didn't bring myself through my hardships — the Lord brought me safely through when I should have died a long time ago.

The Lord showed me that it wasn't my time to die a long time ago because the Lord wasn't finished with me, so He let me live to see this day.

The devil tried to destroy me a long time ago, but he failed and didn't follow through on his plans to kill me.

The Lord foreknew that I would choose to live my life unto Him today.

Even so, the devil is still trying to destroy me, but God has prolonged my life over death and can add on even more years to my life if it's in His holy will.

The devil tried to destroy me a long time ago when I was a little boy who had a heat stroke from playing too much in the summertime heat.

My body was hot and red all over, and someone said they should call the ambulance to take me to the hospital.

The Lord blessed my body to cool off and I didn't have to go to the hospital.

The Lord didn't let the devil destroy me with that heat stroke.

The devil tried to destroy me a long time ago when I was a little boy and fell down the stairs.

I could've broken my neck but the Lord protected me and I only bruised my arm.

The Lord didn't let the devil destroy me a long time ago.

The devil tried to destroy me a long time ago when I was about 12 years old.

There was a big teenage boy who pushed me around and knocked me down several times.

I could have hit my head on something hard and that could have killed me.

The Lord didn't let the devil destroy me.

The devil tried to destroy me a long time ago when I was a newspaper paper carrier at the age of 13.

Two medium-sized dogs tried to attack me while I was riding my bike.

I fought the two dogs and was able to get away from them.

The Lord didn't let the devil destroy me a long time ago.

The devil tried to destroy me a long time ago when I was walking down the street one day in a neighborhood area and two big dogs saw me and ran towards me.

The dogs stopped when they got very close to me.

The Lord spoke to me and told me to stay calm when the dogs sniffed me.

I stayed calm and then the two dogs walked away from me.

The Lord didn't let the devil destroy me a long time ago.

The devil tried to destroy me a long time ago when I was a teenager.

I went to the beach and got caught up in a rip current and I was unable to get out.

I didn't know how to swim and there was no lifeguard around.

The Lord didn't let the devil destroy me — I truly know that today.

I am still alive today because it was the Lord's will for me to be alive today and give my testimony about the bad things that the Lord brought me through.

Those bad things that happened to me a long time ago is like they never happened because of me living my life unto the Lord today.

That long time ago is like a shadow that passed over the landscape.

That long time ago is like waking up out of a bad dream in the early morning sunlight.

That long time ago in my life is like a feather blown away In the wind.

That long time ago went to where the Lord sent it, and that's a place of no return.

The devil tried to destroy me a long time ago because he knew that the Lord could use me to bless someone's life with my testimonies in praise poetry about my Lord and Savior Jesus Christ.

For a long time is like one second to an eternal God who has given me His divine time that I don't deserve to get my life right with Him before it's too late.

It was never too hard for God to bring me this far in my life.

When the devil tried to destroy me a long time ago, God didn't let the devil succeed when I deserved it.

Like a Little Fish Surrounded by Sharks

I was like a little fish surrounded by sharks when I was in the Army at my permanent duty station, Schofield Barracks in Hawaii.

I was 18 years old and inexperienced compared to a lot of the other older soldiers who were very well experienced in their jobs.

I only had a little experience from basic training, compared to the Vietnam War veterans who were all over the barracks where I lived.

I felt like a little fish surrounded by sharks every day.

At my permanent duty station, I had to run three miles, five days a week.

I had to go to the motor pool with some soldiers in my squad to do mechanic work on the dump trucks and jeeps.

I was no mechanic and didn't know how to do that kind of work, but I was surrounded by other soldiers who worked on those vehicles like it was nothing.

There were other soldiers in my company who could drive dump trucks and jeeps, but I could not drive them and didn't have a driver's license.

There were times when I wondered what I had gotten myself into by deciding to become a combat engineer.

When I signed up for the Army, I really didn't know what I was getting myself into.

I didn't know that I would be like a little fish surrounded by sharks.

I know today that the Lord was with me even though I didn't know it at the time.

It was like the wild west where I was stationed in Hawaii.

I hung out with some wild soldiers and experienced things I had never done when I joined the army.

The Lord was with me and protecting me from this wild-wild west.

I was so inexperienced compared to many of the other soldiers, who were from all walks of life all across the nation — there was even a soldier from the Virgin Islands.

My days in the Army were filled with activities.

During the short time I was in the Army, I turned my back on the Lord.

The Lord used two Christian soldiers to try to bring me back to Him, but I didn't care to come back to the Lord at that time.

I took ill and had to be discharged from the Army.

I was like a little fish surrounded by sharks every day, but the Lord didn't let the sharks attack me and eat me up.

I, however, got bitten by some of them because I was so inexperienced and naive in my new environment.

I truly know today that the Lord didn't leave me all alone in my inexperience.

The Lord carried me through when I was like a little fish surrounded by sharks during my short time in the military.

More Than What I Asked Him For

The Lord gave me more than what I asked Him for.

Many years ago, I was discharged from the military with a medical honorable discharge.

I had a nervous breakdown from using some illegal drugs that put me in the hospital for six long months.

The psychiatrist gave me some medicine that caused me to feel numb.

When I took that medicine, I couldn't think about anything at all.

When I took that medicine, I couldn't feel anything at all.

I took the medicine for several years, and I felt nothing that whole time.

Every day was like moving in slow motion to me.

Every day was like a fog in my mind.

Every day was like being in a cold freezer.

The medicine caused me to feel like I was paralyzed every day.

Every day was like a cloudy, rainy day.

Every day was like cold water being poured all over me.

The medicine caused me to feel like I was dead for years and years.

Every day was like time passing by me while I stood still.

Every day was like the sun didn't shine on me.

Every day was like me walking on thin ice.

The medicine caused me to feel like I was trapped in a cage.

Every day was like being locked up in prison.

Every day was like being covered in mud.

One day, I prayed to the Lord to help me cry like other people.

I asked the Lord to help me feel emotional pain like other people.

The Lord spoke to me and said, "I will give you a gold mine of feelings."

The Lord gave me more than what I had asked Him for.

The Lord helped me to stop taking the medicine that made me feel so numb.

That medicine was high in dosage and limited me from doing a lot of things.

Today, I am strong in my mind and stable in my mind because of my Lord and Savior Jesus Christ, who didn't let me stay in my bad condition.

The Lord gave me more than what I asked Him for, even though I didn't think I deserved it.

No one can tell me what the Lord can't do for me, especially since He fixed my broken down mind.

The Lord has truly fixed me up and made me able to write about my past ordeals and share them with others who are not judgmental.

The Lord can give you and me more than what we ask Him for.

He always knows we can use what He gives us to uplift His holy name so we can help others to give God the glory and praise for what He has done for them.

Even After I Got Sick

I was medically honorably discharged from the military, but I still smoked pot and drank alcohol even though I was sick.

I was mentally sick because of smoking some bad marijuana.

After I got sick, I didn't wise up and stop smoking marijuana and drinking beer, wine and liquor.

I smoked marijuana with my girlfriend and drank alcohol like it was a recreation.

I was still sick, but not sick enough to stop what I was doing.

I also smoked marijuana with two of my half-brothers and drank a lot of beer with them too.

I was sick in my mind and at the same time I was able to function normally like everyone else.

Even after I got sick, I was able to still work because my military doctor didn't give me 100% disability.

My military doctor discharged me from the military with a 30% disability, so that I still had to work.

I worked different jobs even though I was sick with the mental condition.

I did normal things just like everyone else.

The people I hung around with didn't treat me like I was sick.

They accepted me for who I was, since I was no trouble to them.

I was sick, but not a troublemaker.

I was sick, but not stupid.

I was sick, but not bad.

My mother knew that I was sick after I was discharged from the military.

My mother knew that I was different from the way I used to be before I got sick, but she didn't change on me just because I was sick mentally.

My mother was good to me and treated me like I wasn't sick.

My step-father and sisters never changed on me either.

They were good to me in my sick condition.

All of my kinfolks were good to me.

They never treated me bad when I was sick mentally.

It didn't even seem like I was sick because they treated me normally.

Even after I got sick, the Lord didn't give up on me.

The Lord foresaw me confessing and repenting of my sins unto Him and living my life unto Him today.

The military doctors had given me life-long medicine to take for my mental sickness.

The Lord gave me the life-long spiritual medicine of His mercy and grace for me to take beyond my mental sickness.

The Lord didn't allow my sickness to get the best of me.

What I Brought on Myself

I must live with what I brought on myself, even though it's not easy.

I brought some hardships on myself through the free will choices I made.

I didn't wait on the Lord to give me the things that I needed.

I did things on my own, of my own free will, and that caused me to suffer.

I deserve to suffer for not putting my trust in the Lord.

I will reap what I sow from the things I brought on myself, and the Lord is not pleased with what I did.

I must face up to what I brought on myself and live with it because the Lord sees what I need to do.

I can't blame the Lord for bringing a hardship on me when I brought it on myself by sinning against Him.

I only cared about my selfish desires and saw no need to confess and repent of my sins that made me truly regret what I brought on myself.

I can't turn back the clock on how I messed up when the Lord didn't interrupt my free will choices that were not good for me and brought hardships on me.

Even though I have confessed and repented of my sins and am living unto the Lord today, I still must reap what I sowed.

It's like me getting badly burned by fire and my wounds taking time to heal.

The hardships that I brought on myself are my wounds and the fire is my bad choices.

The Lord sees fit for me to go through what I brought on myself so that I will truly know what it means to wait on Him.

What I brought on myself was through my own free will which hasn't yet made my life joyful, but doing the Lord's will has made my life joyful beyond what I could bring on myself.

I can't make what I brought on myself disappear like a falling star disappearing in the night sky.

The Lord won't make what I brought on myself disappear, but He will give me the strength to endure it.

During My Time Here on Earth

During my time here on earth, I want to live my life unto the Lord Jesus Christ as if He will come back again during my time.

During my time here on earth, I want to learn from my past mistakes and not make the same mistakes over and over again like I haven't learned anything.

I don't want to live my life unto the devil anymore during my time here on earth.

The devil is all about shortening my time, but Jesus is all about giving me more time on earth to do His will and be saved in Him.

I want to use my time here on earth to love the Lord and love my neighbors every day.

My time on earth is short, but then 100 years of living on earth is short to the Lord, even though it can be long to you and me.

During my time here on earth, I want to be a blessing to my family and church family.

During my time here on earth, I want to be a blessing to the people in my neighborhood.

During my time here on earth, I want to respect everybody and treat everybody right.

During my time here on earth, I want to encourage others to live their lives unto Jesus Christ, my Lord.

During my time here on earth, I want to help everyone I can help.

During my time here on earth, I want to pray for people.

During my time here on earth, I want to live right and set a good example.

During my time here on earth, I want to be saved in Jesus Christ, my Lord and Savior.

During my time here on earth, I want to help other people to be saved in Jesus Christ.

During my time here on earth, I want to give Jesus Christ my best.

During my time here on earth I want to use my talents and spiritual gifts unto the Lord Jesus Christ.

During my time here on earth, I want to give my testimony about all the hardships that Jesus brought me through.

The Lord gives us all our time on Earth — many people's time is longer than others, and many people's time is shorter than others.

During our amount of time on earth, we have enough time to be saved in God's grace.

The Lord gives us all enough time on earth to be saved in Him, who is coming back again at a time that we don't know.

During my time on earth, I want to confess and repent of all of my sins and live my life unto the Lord.

Common Sense Praise Poetry

The Lord has inspired me to write common sense praise poetry so that people can easily understand when they read it.

My testimonies about the Lord are common sense testimonies that are easy to understand.

The Lord has given me common sense to write these praise poems about uplifting and glorifying His holy name.

It takes common sense to know that the sun will rise and set.

It takes common sense to know that the stars will sparkle in the night sky.

It takes common sense to know that the full, white moonlight will glow in the night.

It takes common sense to know that the seasons will change.

It takes common sense to listen when someone is talking.

It takes common sense to take good care of yourself.

It takes common sense to take good care of your children.

It takes common sense to love your wife.

It takes common sense to treat people right.

It takes common sense to talk right.

It takes common sense to do right.

It takes common sense to live right.

I am a common man who loves to write common sense praise poetry about my Lord and Savior Jesus Christ.

Jesus talked to and healed many common people when He lived on earth without sin.

I am glad that Jesus can use a common man like me to be a witness of Him, even to some highly educated people who also have some common sense.

The Lord has blessed my common sense praise poetry to be understood by anyone who is down to earth.

You can see that my praise poetry is down to earth when you read it.

My poetry is plain and simple so that you can understand it and see that my poems are not intellectual praise poetry.

A lot of the English language is made up of common sense words that many people speak every day.

Common people have been around for thousands of years and will never be out of date.

It takes common sense to eat right.

It takes common sense to drink plenty of water.

It takes common sense to drive safely on the road.

It takes common sense to not judge people.

It takes common sense to stay calm in a bad situation.

It takes common sense to take your time to get to know someone.

It takes common sense to not assume things.

It takes common sense to not go out alone in the dark of night.

It takes common sense to not do things in a hurry.

It takes common sense to make plans with the Lord in them.

It takes common sense to respect your husband.

It takes common sense to use your knowledge for good and not evil.

Intellectual poetry is for those who understand it and can relate to it.

Common sense praise poetry is down to earth so that no one will misunderstand.

When Jesus Christ spoke down to earth words many times, he reached people where they were on their level.

I Will Be Happy to See My Jesus

I will be happy to see my Jesus one day when He comes back again on the clouds of glory with all of His angels.

I will be happy to see my Jesus, who helps me to think right every day.

I will be happy to see my Jesus, who helps me to talk right every day.

I will be happy to see my Jesus, who helps me to act right every day.

I will be happy to see my Jesus, who helps me to get a good night's sleep.

I will be happy to see my Jesus, who gives me the strength to get through the day.

I will be happy to see my Jesus, who is there for me all of the time.

I will be happy to see my Jesus, who lifts me up when I'm feeling down.

I will be happy to see my Jesus, who motivates me.

I will be happy to see my Jesus, who encourages me.

I will be happy to see my dead loved ones, when Jesus comes back again.

Seeing my dead loved ones again will be good but not as great as seeing my Jesus, who brought me through hardships that no one else could.

I will be happy to see my Jesus, who will never let me down.

I will be happy to see my Jesus, who gives me joy.

I will be happy to see my Jesus, who spared my life from death for me to see this day.

I will be happy to see my Jesus, who understands me completely.

I will be happy to see my Jesus, who keeps me strong.

I will be happy to see my Jesus, who loves me more than anyone else in this world.

I will be happy to see my Jesus, who never fails me.

I will be happy to see my Jesus, who I can always talk to.

I will be happy to see my Jesus, who I can always trust.

I will be happy to see my Jesus, who is my best friend.

I will be happy to see my Jesus, who will never leave me or forsake me.

I will be happy to see my Jesus, who will be happy to see me when He comes back again.

Jesus will be happy to see everyone who will go back with Him to heaven.

I will be happy to see my Jesus, who answers my prayers.

I will be happy to see my Jesus, who forgives me of my sins.

I will be happy to see my Jesus, who cleanses me from my sins.

I will be happy to see my Jesus, who saved me from my sins.

I will be happy to see my Jesus, who died on the cross for my sins.

I will be happy to see my Jesus, who rose from the grave to give me eternal life.

I will be happy to see my Jesus, who redeems me back to God.

I will be happy to see my Jesus when He comes back again.

I will be happy to see my Jesus, who never lied to me.

I will be happy to see my Jesus, you will never hurt my heart.

I will be happy to see my Jesus, who will never do me wrong.

I will be happy to see my Jesus, who will never control me.

I will be happy to see my Jesus Christ, who gave me a free will to choose to love Him or not love Him.

I will be happy to see my Jesus, who always tells me the truth in love.

I will be happy to see my Jesus, who gives me peace of mind.

I will be happy to see my Jesus, who works out all of my problems.

I will be happy to see my Jesus, who will never change on me.

I will be happy to see my Jesus, who won't put more on me than what I can bear.

The Creator of All Existence

The Creator of all existence is beyond a billion good dreams that the Lord Jesus Christ can make come true.

The Creator of all existence is beyond a billion imaginations that can't ever imagine all of the things that Jesus Christ has for us up in heaven.

The Creator of all existence is beyond a billion health messages that don't come close to Jesus Christ's tree of life that is up in heaven for you and me to eat from if we make it to heaven.

The Creator of all existence is beyond a million technologies that are like broken glass when compared to Jesus Christ, who will create a new heaven and a new earth with technologies reaching to other worlds in other universes.

The Creator of all existence is beyond all the people who ever existed in this world that Jesus created.

All the living and all of the dead can never add up to the number of stars that Jesus created in the outer space.

The Creator of all existence is beyond all existence, which is like a small mustard seed compared to the unmeasurable God, Father, Son and Holy Spirit, who are too big for the heavens to hold.

The Lord God downsized Himself to a small, tiny man to save you and me from our sins.

The Lord Doesn't Forget Us

One day, I went out to the store to buy something that I wanted to eat.

When I went inside the store, I saw one of my neighbors who lives in my community.

She didn't see me inside the store when I walked by her.

When I left the store, I was walking toward my car when I saw my neighbor again about thirty feet away from me.

I saw her looking for her car with her car remote in her hand.

She was pressing the buttons on her car remote, trying to find her car.

I looked over and said to her, "Here is your car; it was parked right behind my car in the store's parking lot and as she was pressing the button on her car remote, I could see the car's parking lights blinking.

She thanked me for letting her know where her car was parked.

You and I can thank the Lord for not forgetting to come back again to this world to take all of His righteous children to Heaven.

The Lord doesn't forget us, even though we can sometimes forget where we put things.

The only thing that the Lord will forget is our confessed and repented sins, which He will wipe away as though we never sinned against Him.

The Lord doesn't forget you and me and leave us all alone without warning us of the results of our bad choices in life.

The Lord is good to us all the time, and the Lord doesn't forget to give us His salvation, even though we can forget that sometimes before we deny ourselves, pick up our crosses and follow Jesus Christ.

Life Said to Death

Life said to Death, you can't get rid of me — I've was around before you ever existed.

Life said to Death, I kicked you out of heaven, which I filled with eternal life to be forever youthful beyond you, O Death.

Life said to Death, no matter how hard you try to get rid of me that will never happen because I am life that will be here until Jesus Christ comes back again.

Life said to Death, no sickness will be able to get rid of me.

No war will be able to get rid of me.

No virus or disease will be able to get rid of me.

No crime will be able to get rid of me.

No flood will be able to get rid of me.

No hurricane will be able to get rid of me.

No earthquake will be able to get rid of me.

No tornado or wildfire will be able to get rid of me.

Life said to Death, no nuclear bombs will be able to get rid of me.

No accident will be able to get rid of me.

No riot I will be able to get rid of me.

Life said to Death, I will throw you in the Lake of fire one day, and you will burn up and turn to ash while I live on forever and ever.

Life said to Death, you can't ever get rid of me, but I will get rid of you through Jesus Christ, who gives me the victory over you, O Death.

Life said to Death, you have lied to and deceived so many people who I give life to live for Jesus Christ.

Life said to Death, I have my people who will not believe your lies and deceptions because they love to live their lives unto Jesus Christ, who is my life eternal.

Life said to Death, I will still exist when you, O Death, will one day disappear from the planet earth like you never existed.

Life said to Death, you will not exist in the new earth where I will live in all of God's children who will trample all over death like crushing up dried leaves that have fallen from the trees.

Life said to Death, I am eternal and you, O Death, are temporary and will be gone forever and ever one day.

Life said to Death, I am from God, no matter how many people you take with you to the grave.

Life said to Death, I have my people who you can't deceive into believing that their lives are so vain.

They know that living for Jesus Christ is an abundance of life that will lead them to receive eternal life one day.

Life said to Death, so many people are afraid of you all around the world, but my people are not afraid of you because they know that they will live again when Jesus Christ comes back.

Life said to Death, my people know how to pray away their fear of you, O Death.

Life said to Death, you can take my people to the grave, but you can't keep them there because Jesus will raise them from the grave as if you never existed, O Death.

Life said to Death, your time will soon be up and you will be thrown in the lake of fire and brimstone where even all the wicked will know too late that life lives on in Jesus Christ.

Life said to Death, you tried to get rid of me thousands of years ago and you failed to do so in the Garden of Eden.

Adam and Eve chose you, O Death over me, but God didn't let them die without populating the earth with their lifeblood children.

Life said to Death, I was here yesterday, I am here today and I will still be here tomorrow, beyond whoever will die.

Life said to Death, you can't get rid of me, no matter how many times you, O Death, dodge in and out of the lanes of time that will eventually crush you.

Life said to Death, I existed before your evolution and Big Bang Theory that didn't create me — I am a theory only in the minds of atheists who I give life to live with their lies.

Life said to Death, I am looking forward to giving eternal life to all who are saved in Jesus Christ, who gives me life eternal over you, who can't fill up the grave like God filling up the Heavens with life that the holy angels know to be real forever and ever.

Life said to Death, I will give life to many more babies, no matter how many people you swallow down in the grave.

Life said to Death, you can't outdo God, who is eternal life beyond you, O Death, you are doomed to never walk through the gates of heaven that my holy and righteous people will one day walk through because of Jesus Christ.

Life said to Death, none of your schemes and devices will be able to get rid of me because I am life, who is still here through thousands of years of your presence, O Death.

Your presence, O Death, is not strong enough to get rid of me.

Life said to Death, you can't get rid of me, no matter how ignorant, unjust and negligent you are, O Death.

Life said to Death, you will never overpower me and get rid of me off the face of this world.

The devil and his fallen angels and his human agents believe that you, O Death, can get rid of me.

Life said to Death, you were already defeated when Jesus Christ died on the cross and rose from the grave with victory over you.

Life said to death, you couldn't keep Jesus in the grave because Jesus is eternal life and will destroy you, O Death, one day in the lake of fire and brimstone.

It's up to You and Me to Obey God's Call

God calls you and me out of the spiritual Babylon that is all about religious confusion that has been going on for thousands of years on earth.

The Lord God called me out of going to church on Sunday, which many people believed to be God's holy Sabbath day of rest.

I obeyed God's call and came in to The Seventh-Day Adventist Church that preaches and teaches all the Bible truth.

The Seventh Day Adventist Church doesn't add any words to or take any words out of the Holy Bible.

It's up to you and me to obey God's call when God calls everybody out of the spiritual Babylon that the devil loves to spread around the world.

God says that He has other sheep that are not in his fold.

There are many true faithful people who go to church on Sunday, and God will call them out and they will obey His call to come to The Seventh-Day Adventist Church just like I did when God called me out of going to church on Sunday.

Saturday is the seventh day of the week, and is the holy Sabbath day of rest to worship God in spirit and truth.

There is no truth in observing Sunday to be the holy Sabbath day of rest.

It's not written in the Bible that Sunday is the seventh day of the week to be observed as the holy Sabbath day of rest.

It's up to you and me to obey God's call to come out of the spiritual Babylon that's all about religious confusion that the Seventh Day Adventist Church doesn't preach and teach to the world.

The Bible says that the truth will set you free, and the Bible is all truth about God's will for everyone to come out of religious confusion that will preach and teach false doctrines that are not written in God's holy word.

I am so glad today that I chose to obey God's call for me to come to the Seventh-day Adventist Church that keeps all the Ten Commandments of God.

The Seventh Day Adventist Church doesn't preach and teach any false doctrines, like when you die you go straight to heaven and look down on the people in this world.

That is not written in the Bible, which says that Jesus Christ is coming back again to raise the righteous dead and take them to heaven with the righteous living.

Religious confusion is of the devil, who doesn't want you and me to believe all the truth in the Bible.

The devil deceived Eve and made her believe his lie that sounded so religious, but was not true and was the beginning of religious confusion here on earth.

The devil's religious confusion truly began in heaven where Lucifer was spreading around his false doctrines to the other angels and causing a rebellion against God.

Jesus Christ reminded the angels of all of God's truth, but one-third of the angels rejected God's truth and were kicked out of heaven.

It's up to you and me to obey God's call.

We have a free will choice to obey God's call, just like two-thirds of the angels in heaven obeyed God's call for them to live by all of God's truth.

If There is No God

If there is no God, there is no love.

If God didn't exist, then love wouldn't exist.

God is love, forever and ever.

There would be no love in this world if there was no God.

The reason why a man can love his wife is because of God, who is where love comes from.

Love is of God.

Love is from God.

No one can love if there is no God, who is love.

Parents wouldn't love their children if there was no God.

The devil is not love, because the devil is full of hate all the time.

God is full of love all the time.

It would be a strange act of God to destroy what He created.

Love would not exist at all if there was no God.

Those who don't believe in God won't reject love, because it makes them feel good when they are falling in love — what they don't realize is that it's God's love they're feeling.

If there is no God, there is no love in anyone, even in the animals that can love you and me because God is love.

If anyone says that there is no God, they are truly saying that there is no love, even when they exist because of God, who is love.

Many people don't believe in God, but they believe in love and try to find their true love.

Many wicked people will love their children and won't kill their children because love is stronger than hate.

God is love that is stronger than wickedness, and wickedness can't stop God from loving sinners like you and me.

If there is no God, no one would be able to love themselves.

You and I can't love ourselves if we don't love God.

It's You and God Alone

It's you and God alone in your heart, where only God sees your motives.

It's you and God alone in your heart, where only God sees your intentions.

It's you and God alone in your mind, where only God sees your thoughts.

You can be with your husband and feel alone.

You can be with your wife and feel alone.

You can be with your children and feel alone.

You can be on your job and feel alone.

You can be in a crowd and feel alone.

You can be in church and feel alone.

You can be with your girlfriend and feel alone.

You can be with your boyfriend and feel alone.

You can be with your pets and feel alone.

You can be in the store and feel alone.

It's you and God alone, even when you go to a football and basketball game and other people are sitting down all around you.

You must face God alone in your heart, which might be full of bad motives and intentions.

You must face God alone in your mind, which might be full of evil thoughts.

It's you and God alone, and no one else can answer to God for you in your sins or in your faithfulness and obedience unto Him.

You and I can feel all alone, but we can pray to God and be with Him.

You and I can be with others, but that can't change the fact that we must face God all alone.

It's you and God alone every day in your soul's salvation.

It's you and God alone, and Jesus Christ is God to be alone with you and judge you.

If I

If I help you, I help myself.

If I encourage you, I encourage myself.

If I don't forgive you, I don't forgive myself.

If I love you, I love myself.

If I hate you, I hate myself.

If I lie to you, I lie to myself.

If I tell you the truth, I tell myself the truth.

If I respect you, I respect myself.

If I cheat you, I cheat myself.

If I despise you, I despise myself.

If I trouble you, I trouble myself.

If I am good to you, I am good to myself.

If I am at peace with you, I am at peace with myself.

If I hurt your heart, I hurt my heart.

If I pretend with you, I pretend with myself.

The Lord says to love thy neighbor as thyself.

The Lord didn't say love thyself as thy neighbor.

When the Lord said put thy neighbor before thyself, you must love thy neighbor to love thyself.

You can't love thyself if you don't love thy neighbor.

You and I must put others before ourselves.

Most of all, if I love God, I love myself.

I must love God and my neighbor before I love myself.

If I do you right, I do myself right.

If I do you wrong, I do myself wrong.

If I am fair to you, I am fair to myself.

If I am happy for you, I am happy for myself.

If I am mean to you, I am mean to myself.

If I am kind to you, I am kind to myself.

If I am gentle with you, I am gentle with myself.

God says to love thy neighbor as thyself.

You and I must put thy neighbor ahead of ourselves, and most of all we must put the Lord God Jesus Christ ahead of ourselves.

What the Lord says is very profound to you and me, because we can't swallow down what the Lord says if we are selfish and do not love our neighbors.

For Free

Many people are not used to people giving them something good for free.

Many people will look at you and me like we are out of our minds if we give them something good for free.

Many people are used to buying things.

Many people are used to people trying to sell them something.

There are some people who are happy about what you give them free of charge.

There are some people who won't even say thank you after you've given them something for free.

Many people will look at you and me like we are crazy for giving them something good for free.

Many people will look at you and me like we are stupid for giving them something good for free.

Many people will look at you and me like we are weak for giving them something good for free.

Many people will talk bad about you and me for giving them something good for free.

Some church folks will look at you and me like something is wrong with us for giving them something good for free.

Church folks know that there is nothing wrong with the Lord for giving them His blessings for free, but some church folks will look at you and me like we have lost our minds for giving them something good for free.

Selfish people don't understand when generous people give something for free.

Selfish people believe that generous people must have an ulterior motive for giving them something for free.

Selfish people can't relate to generous people because when a selfish person gives you and me something good for free there's a bad motive behind it.

When generous people give people something good for free, it lifts them up and brightens their days.

When a selfish person gives people something good for free, there is trouble on the way because they will want something in return.

The Lord gives everyone life, health and strength for free, and no one in their right mind would look at the Lord like He is crazy for giving them these things.

When you and I give people something good for free, some people will question it and judge it to be something wrong because they can't relate to giving people something good for free.

All good things are from the Lord, so when generous people give you something good for free, it's really from the Lord.

What God Joins Together

What God has join together, let no man put asunder.

What God has join together, let no woman put asunder.

What God has join together, let no dream put asunder.

What God has join together, let no disagreements put asunder.

What God has join together, let no children put asunder.

What God has join together, let no education put asunder.

What God has join together, let no job put asunder.

What God has join together, let no wealth put asunder.

What God has join together, let no poverty put asunder.

What God has join together, let no animal put asunder.

What God has join together, let no Pride put asunder.

What God has join together, let no trials put asunder.

What God has join together, let no aging put asunder.

What God has join together, let no sickness put asunder.

What God has join together, let no misfortune put asunder.

What God has join together, let no assuming put asunder.

What God has join together, let no time put asunder.

What God has join together, let no career put asunder.

What God has join together, let no government put asunder.

What God has join together, let no state put under.

What God has join together, let no country put asunder.

What God has join together, let no war put asunder.

What God has join together is meant to stay together.

What God has joined together is no mistake and is meant to be together.

What you and I join together will be a mistake.

What you and I join together will not always stay together.

What you and I join together will cause us to regret it.

What you and I join together will give us some heartaches.

What you and I join together can be abusive.

What you and I join together can be trouble.

What you and I join together can be deadly.

What God has join together, let no grief put asunder.

God will not join an incompatible man and woman together.

God will join together a man and woman who will love and obey Him.

God will join together a man and woman who love each other till death do they part.

If you and I put our own marriage together, we will sooner or later regret it in some kind of way.

The Bible says that if an unbelieving spouse is pleased to stay in the marriage and treat you and me right, the Lord can bless the marriage even though you and I put together our own marriage.

It's always good to wait on the Lord to bless you with your soulmate to take as your husband or wife for life.

What you and I join together can bring on fear.

What you and I join together can bring on selfishness.

What you and I join together can bring on unforgiveness.

What God joins together, let no one and no thing put asunder.

I Don't Mean to Burst Your Bubble

I don't mean to burst your bubble, but when you die, you don't go straight to heaven.

You won't go to heaven before Jesus Christ comes back again.

Jesus Christ is coming back again to raise the righteous dead and take the righteous living back to heaven with Him and all the Angels.

When Jesus takes you and me back to heaven, we will have a bodily form and we will not have a spirit floating out in the air.

I don't mean to burst your bubble, but evolution didn't create the universe and this world — God created the universe and this world.

Evolution didn't create human beings and the animals — God created a man and a woman and all the animals.

I don't mean to burst your bubble, but when we die we won't go to a place between heaven and hell.

God created heaven and God created hell, but God didn't create anything in-between heaven and hell for you and me to go to where we can get a final chance to be saved or lost.

Now is our chance to be saved or lost, while we live in this world today.

I don't mean to burst your bubble, but if you read the Bible you will see that I am telling you the truth because the Bible is not a fairytale book.

I don't mean to burst your bubble, but you will reap what you sow for believing the devil's lie.

I don't mean to burst your bubble, but there is a God and the devil knows that to be true, but he doesn't want you and me to believe that there is a God.

I don't mean to burst your bubble, but you can't blame God for the death of a loved one.

God is all about giving life, which the devil loves to take away.

I don't mean to burst your bubble, but you can't question God about anything.

God made Job look foolish when Job questioned God, and God questioned Job by saying, "Where were you when I laid the earth's foundation?"

I don't mean to burst your bubble, but you can't talk to the dead, because they can't hear you and can't see you.

It's the fallen angels who appear to be your dead loved ones.

Those demons can talk to you and make you believe that it's your dead loved ones appearing before you.

The Bible says that the dead know nothing.

Bewitched

Sin can bewitch us, because sin can look so good in our eyes.

We can look at sin and not even realize what we are looking at it.

Sin can bewitch us and make us accept it like it's a good thing.

Sin can bewitch us and make us overlook it being a bad thing.

Sin has bewitched so many people and made them glorify sin.

Sin has bewitched so many people and made them love sinning against the Lord.

Sin has bewitched many church folks into accepting sin as a moral thing.

Sin has bewitched many church folks and made them cherish sin in their lives.

Sin will be with you and me if we don't keep our eyes on Jesus Christ.

If we keep our eyes on immortality, sin will bewitch us.

If we accept anything and everything, then sin will bewitch us.

Sin has bewitched many church folks and made them be of the world.

Sin has bewitched many church folks and made them dress like the people of the world.

Sin can bewitch anyone who doesn't see sin to be what God hates.

God loves the sinner and wants to save him or her from being lost in sin.

Sin is breaking God's holy law.

Anyone who breaks God's holy law is bewitched by sin that can very often look so good but be so deadly as to kill us.

O Lord, You Kept Today's Technology Away

O Lord, you kept today's technology away from those people back in the Bible days.

O Lord, if you had allowed today's technology to exist back in the Bible days, many people would have worshipped this technology.

Many people would have believed in today's technology and not believed in You, O Lord.

O Lord, you have created many people who were brilliant and skillful back in the Bible days.

Many of them would have used their brilliance and skillfulness to greatly advance this technology so that they could rule the world with it.

O Lord, you kept today's technology away from the people back in the Bible days.

Many kings back in the Bible days would have used today's technology to greatly oppress many people.

The technology back in the Bible days caused many kings to be very proud.

If they had today's technology, they would have been a lot prouder about building up their kingdoms.

Many kings back in the Bible days would have probably used today's technology to annihilate every nation that was against them.

Jesus Christ came to this world during the darkest days on earth, when so many people were rebellious against God.

If they had today's technology back in the Bible days, they would have been a lot more rebellious.

They would have probably believed that they were more powerful than God if they had today's technology.

Many people back in the Bible days would probably not have believed in Jesus Christ if they had today's technology.

Many people back in the Bible days would have probably believed that there is no God if they had today's technology.

Many people today believe that there is no God because they put their trust in today's technology.

Many people today worship technology like it's God.

Many people back in the Bible days would have probably been much worse off and living their lives unto today's technology just like many people live their lives today.

Oh Lord, you kept today's technology away from the people back in the Bible days.

If this world will still be here another thousand years, the Lord will keep that thousand years technology away from you and me today because the Lord knows that we would probably worship that new thousand years technology if we had it now.

The Lord doesn't overdo anything that would cause this world's past, present and future to be out of order with time.

It wasn't the time for the people back in the Bible days to have today's technology and it's not our time to have the technology of one thousand years in the future.

The Lord kept today's technology away from the people back in the Bible days because the Lord keeps technology, as well as science, in its rightful place.

Your All and All

Why make education your all and all, when education won't be useful to you when you die and go to the grave where you will wake up one day in the first or second resurrection.

Why make technology your all and all, when technology won't be useful to you when you die and go to the grave where you will wake up one day in the first or second resurrection.

Why make science your all and all, when science won't be useful to you when you die and go to the grave and wake up one day in the first or second resurrection.

You will hope that you will wake up in the first resurrection for being saved in Jesus Christ.

You and I must give our all and all to the Lord Jesus Christ so that we can wake up in the first resurrection where education, technology and science will be eternal because God is our highest education, our highest technology and our highest science that this world can't comprehend.

Talents

God gives everybody talents, but there are many people who are proud of their talents and only think about themselves rising up to the top.

Many people will worship their talents and not worship God, who has given them their talents.

Our talents are a good thing if we use them for the Lord.

Our talents can be a bad thing if we use them for selfish reasons.

God gives everybody talents for His glory, not for us to use our talents for ourselves.

Many people will let their talents go to their heads.

They get a swelled head if their talents get them a lot of attention.

They get a swelled head if their talents give them a good paying job.

They get a swelled head if their talents cause them to make many friends.

They get a swelled head if their talents make them rich and famous.

God gives everybody talents to be used to please Him, not to please themselves.

Talents are not to be used for selfish ambitions.

Talents are to be used for spreading the Gospel of Jesus Christ all around the world.

Everybody has the right

Everybody has the right to believe what they want to believe.

Everybody has the right to say what they want to say.

Everybody has the right to do what they want to do.

Everybody has the right to go where they want to go.

Everybody has the right to eat what they want to eat.

Everybody has the right to drink what they want to drink.

Everybody has the right to live where they want to live.

Beyond the rights that everybody has, no one will have regrets for believing in Jesus Christ.

Beyond the rights that everybody has, no one will have regrets for speaking words about Jesus Christ.

Beyond the rights that everybody has, no one will have regrets for doing the Lord's will.

Beyond the rights that everybody has, no one will have regrets for eating the right Foods unto the Lord.

Beyond the rights that everyone has, no one will have regrets for drinking the liquids unto the Lord.

Beyond the rights that everybody has, no one will have regrets for going where the Lord's presence lives.

Beyond the rights that everybody has, no one will have regrets for living where the Lord is pleased to have us live.

Everybody has their rights, but no one will have regrets for living right unto the Lord Jesus Christ.

Tell Your Truth

Tell your truth, because your truth can help someone else.

Tell your truth, because your truth can encourage someone else.

Tell your truth, because your truth can open up someone else's eyes.

Tell your truth, because your truth can set someone else free.

Tell your truth, because your truth can help someone else go the extra mile.

Tell your truth, because your truth can cause someone else to feel better.

Tell your truth, because your truth can light up someone else's life.

Tell your truth, because your truth can help someone else to regret doing something wrong.

Tell your truth, because your truth can help someone else to regret saying something wrong.

Tell your truth, because your truth can change someone else's life.

Tell your truth, because your truth can help someone else to wise up.

Tell your truth, because your truth can make someone else strong.

Tell your truth, because your truth can help someone else to not be confused.

Tell your truth, because your truth can get someone else's full attention.

Tell your truth, because your truth can cheer someone else up.

Tell your truth, because your truth can make someone else think twice before doing something wrong.

Tell your truth, because your truth can help someone else go far in life.

Tell your truth, because your truth can turn someone else's world around.

Of Every Sin in Our Lives

We must confess and repent of every sin in our lives.

We have seen sins and we have unseen sins, and we must confess and repent of every seen sin in our lives.

Even one sin that we hold onto will cause our souls to be lost.

Even one sin in our lives can control you and me if we don't confess and repent of that one sin.

Only Jesus Christ can give us the power to overcome our sins that He will cleanse us from.

We should never take any pleasure in holding onto our sins, because doing that will mean the sins will sooner or later possess our souls.

We must stay in prayer every day so that the devil will not tempt you and me to sin against God.

The devil hates to see you and me asking God to forgive us of our sins because he loves to fill our hearts with lustful desires that will cause us to be lost in our sins.

We must confess and repent of every sin that we are aware of so that we know our weaknesses have no power over our minds.

If we don't pray to Jesus to give us strength, our weaknesses and sins will overpower our minds.

Our flesh is weak to sin against the Lord at any time of the day, when our minds should be on the Lord.

We were born in sin for even our senses to give in to sin without you and me realizing it.

We need to confess and repent of every sin in our lives, which belong to the Lord, not you and me.

Sin will destroy our souls and send us to hell that God created for the devil and his fallen angels.

We can never take sin lightly because sin will keep on coming back at us if we don't pray for the Lord to take it away.

We must always stay in prayer because as long as we live, the devil will tempt us to sin against the Lord who overcame every sin for you and me to choose not to willfully sin against Him.

It's Sad to See

It's sad to see loved ones leave the church.

It's sad to see church members leave the church.

When they leave the church, they leave the Lord heartbroken after all He has done for them.

They leave you and me greatly disappointed and confused about why they stopped coming to church to worship the Lord.

They will go to work and will go anywhere else, except for going to church where they truly need to be just like you and me.

It's hard to see people leaving the church and turning their backs on Jesus Christ, as well as turning their backs on you and me who must hold onto Jesus on the good days and the bad days.

When people leave the church, it takes something out of you and me if we love them like we are supposed to do in the church and outside of the church.

It's sad to see anyone leaving the church, Jesus Christ and you and me.

To leave Jesus means they are leaving the spiritual life that is the best life to live every day in this world where it's sad to see people lost in their sins if we love them like Jesus loves them.

It's especially sad to see loved ones not being in the church to worship the Lord and Savior Jesus Christ.

Hold it Together

O Lord, You hold protons together.

O Lord, You hold electrons together.

O Lord, You hold neutrons together.

O Lord, You hold my dreams together.

O Lord, You hold my body parts together.

O Lord, You hold my life together.

O Lord, You hold the ground together.

O Lord, You hold the sky together.

O Lord, You hold the stars together.

O Lord, You hold the world together.

O Lord, You hold nations together.

O Lord, You hold governments together.

O Lord, You hold the universe together.

O Lord, You hold the church together.

O Lord, You hold nature together.

O Lord, You hold the visible together.

O Lord, You hold the invisible together.

O Lord, You hold the deep oceans together.

O Lord, You hold faith in You together.

O Lord, You hold all existence together.

O Lord, You hold truth together.

O Lord, You hold mercy together.

O Lord, You hold grace together.

O Lord, You hold peace together.

O Lord, You hold health together.

O Lord, You hold joy together.

O Lord, You hold the heavens together.

O Lord, all that You hold together will never fall apart.

No man can hold together what You, O Lord, can hold together.

O Lord, You hold the days together.

O Lord, You hold the nights together.

O Lord, You hold the years together.

O Lord, You hold the seasons together.

O Lord, You hold Your holy words together.

Man cannot hold himself together.

The angels cannot hold themselves together.

Lucifer the fallen angels proved that to be true.

O Lord, You hold justice together.

O Lord, You hold fairness together.

O Lord, You hold eternal life together.

O Lord You hold the living together.

O Lord, You hold the grave together.

O Lord, You hold your children together.

If We Make Excuses

If we make excuses for our sins, we have no faith in Jesus Christ.

If we make excuses for our sins, we are playing church.

If we make excuses for our sins, we don't know Jesus Christ.

If we make excuses for our sins, we don't have the Holy Spirit.

If we make excuses for our sins, we won't confess and repent of our sins.

If we make excuses for our sins, we are spiritually blind.

If we make excuses for our sins, we are not Christians.

If we know that we do wrong and make excuses for our wrongs, we have no renewed life in Jesus Christ.

If we say something wrong and own up to it, there is hope that we will change for the better.

If we do something wrong and own up to it, the Lord can help us to do better.

If we make excuses for our sins, we are downright foolish.

If we make excuses for our sins, the truth is not in us.

If we make excuses for our sins, the Lord will be against us.

If we make excuses for our sins, we are better off to have never been born.

If we make excuses for our sins, we are lost in our sins.

If we make excuses for our sins, our lives are worthless and we have no reason to exist.

God will never excuse our sins, no matter what reasons we have or excuses we make for them.

No sin is too hard for the Lord to cleanse us from.

If we make excuses for our sins, we are telling the Lord that He is not strong enough to help us to overcome our weaknesses.

If we make excuses for our sins, we are showing the Lord that His death on the cross was worthless.

If we make excuses for our sins, we are telling the Lord Jesus Christ that He didn't get the victory over all of our sins for us to be saved in Him.

If we make excuses for our sins, we are only fooling ourselves and surely not God.

If we make excuses for our sins, we are of the devil and not of God.

You Can Usually Tell

You can usually tell if you have a good effect on people because they will be glad to see you. You can usually tell if people like you because they will be glad to invite you into their homes.

You can usually tell if people love you because if you need their help, they will be glad to help you.

You can usually tell who is a friend to you because he or she will tell you the truth.

You can usually tell if people are good or bad by the way they treat you.

You can usually tell if people are Christians by the way they behave themselves.

You can usually tell if people are intelligent or stupid by the way they speak.

You can usually tell if you are doing your best because you will be satisfied with what you do.

You can usually tell that God is real by what you see God doing for you in your life.

I Need You to Help Me

I need You to help me to love you, my Lord.

I need You to help me love my neighbors, my Lord.

I need you to help me love myself, my Lord.

I need You to help me to take good care of myself, my Lord.

I need You to help me to take good care of my pets, my Lord.

I need You to help me to drive safely on the local roads and highways, my Lord.

I need You to help me to make good choices, my Lord.

I need You to help me to live right unto You, my Lord.

I need You to help me to think right, my Lord.

I need You to help me talk right, my Lord.

I need You to help me to do right, my Lord.

I need You to help me to help myself, my Lord.

I need You to help me to help someone else, my Lord.

I need You to help me to pray to You, my Lord.

I need You to help me to do Your holy will, my Lord.

I need You to help me to work out my own soul's salvation, my Lord.

I need You to help me to examine myself, my Lord and Savior Jesus Christ.

I need You to help me to trust You, my Lord.

I need You to help me to depend on You, my Lord.

I need You to help me to deny myself and pick up my cross and follow You, my Lord.

I need You to help me to humble myself onto You, my Lord.

I need You to help me to have faith in You every day, my Lord.

I need You to help me to obey You every day, my Lord.

I need You to help me to study Your holy word, my Lord.

I need You to help me to live by Your holy word, my Lord.

I need You to help me to go to church, my Lord.

I need You to help me to worship You, my Lord.

I need You to help me to give You the glory and praise, my Lord.

I need You to help me to confess and repent of my sins, my Lord.

I need You to help me to tell the truth, my Lord.

I need You to help me to not stray away from You, my Lord.

I need You to help me to love my enemies, my Lord.

I need You to help me to forgive others, my Lord.

I need You to help me to forgive myself, my Lord.

There are People Who will Only Love You

There are people who will only love you if you're educated like them.

There are people who will only love you if you are successful like them.

There are people who will only love you if you're rich like them.

There are people who will only love you if you are brilliant like them.

There are people who will only love you if you are intelligent like them.

There are people who will only love you if you are skillful like them.

There are people who will only love you if you can do what they can do.

There are people who will only love you if you are good like them.

There are people who will only love you if you are bad like them.

There are people who will only love you if you are smart like them.

There are people who will only love you if you are wise like them.

There are people who will only love you if you are foolish like them.

There are people who will only love you if you're healthy like them.

There are people who will only love you if you are cheerful like them.

There are people who will only love you if you are judgmental like them.

There are people who will only love you if you are prejudiced like them.

There are people who will only love you if you work hard like them.

There are people who will only love you if you are happy like them.

There are people who will only love you if you are proud like them.

There are people who will only love you if you are deceptive like them.

There are people who will only love you if you are real like them.

There are people who will only love you if you are knowledgeable like them.

There are people who will only love you if you're talented like them.

There are people who will only love you if you are gifted like them.

There are people who will only love you if you are popular like them.

There are people who will only love you if you are strong like them.

There are people who will only love you if you are beautiful like them.

There are people who will only love you if you go to church like them.

There are people who will only love you if you are a leader in the church like them.

There are people who will only love you if you gossip like them.

There are people who will only love you if you talk a lot like them.

There are people who will only love you if you are mean like them.

There are people who will only love you if you are lovable like them.

There are people who will only love you if you are polite like them.

There are people who will only love you if you are encouraging like them.

There are people who will only love you if you are friendly like them.

There are people who will only love you if you are determined like them.

There are people who will only love you if you are cautious like them.

War

A good nation will not go to war with another good nation.

War is about a bad nation wanting to fight a good nation.

War can also be about a bad nation wanting to fight another bad nation.

Controlling people are bad people who want to start wars with anyone they can't control.

A good nation will fight in a war to protect its good people from a bad nation of people.

Most wars are about bad leaders in a nation wanting to control a good nation's people who have good leaders.

War is about a nation of greedy people who want to take away the rights of content people in another nation.

War is about a nation of covetous people who want to take away the wealth of another nation.

Many innocent people suffer and die because of selfish leaders in bad nations.

The very first war was in heaven, when Lucifer wanted what belonged to God.

Lucifer coveted God's creations and His holy throne.

Lucifer and his angels lost the war in heaven because Lucifer had no chance to win the war against God.

Good nations are blessed by God, and bad nations will get envious of good nations and want to start a war with them.

Bad nations love to control their own people to keep their bad laws.

Good nations give their people the freedom to prosper, but bad nations oppress their own people.

The only good thing that comes out of war is that a good nation wins the war and keeps its people safe from being oppressed by a bad nation.

A God-fearing nation will not start a war with any other nation, but a rebellious nation will seek out other nations to fight because they want to control them.

Black Love

Black love is like the sun rising in the east and setting in the west.

Black love is like the full moonlight glowing all night long.

Black love is like all the shining stars in the universe.

Black love is like the great blue sky hovering over this world.

Black love is like climbing the highest mountain to get to the top.

Black love is like walking down in the valley to see the beautiful lilies in the valley.

Black love is like submerging down in the deepest ocean to explore the ocean floor.

Black love is like the beautiful green grass that you and I can lay down on.

Black love is like the birds building their nests on the treetops.

Black love is like solving a deep mystery.

Black love is like a beautiful song.

Black love is like a warm, gentle breeze.

Black love is like a campfire burning all night long.

Black love is like the rain showers.

Black love is like the beautiful white snowflakes.

Black love is like moving into a brand-new house.

Black love is like buying a brand-new car.

Black love is like drinking some clean, fresh water.

Black love is like a treasure chest full of gold.

Black love is like a river that flows into the ocean.

Black love is like getting a good night's sleep.

Black love is like being rich.

Black love is like a very beautiful woman.

Black love is like a beautiful wedding.

Black love is like beautiful furniture.

Black love is like a cruise ship sailing on the ocean waters.

Black love is like a beautiful picture in a beautiful frame.

Black love is like a best-selling book.

Black love is like the beautiful countryside.

Black love is like a high tower.

Black love is like a very secure vault in the bank.

Black love is like eating healthy food.

Black love is like a beautiful, sunny, warm day.

Black love is like a beautiful quiet night.

Black love is like a picnic in the park.

Black love is like a lighthouse shining over the ocean waters in the dark night.

Black love is like eating a fresh-baked sweet potato pie.

Black love is like getting a good education.

Black love is like making a new discovery.

Black love is like a beautiful black stallion.

Black love is like a trip around the world.

Black Love is like heaven on earth.

Black love is like a beautiful waterfall.

Black love is like a righteous nation winning the war.

Black love is like the sun shining through a big house.

Black love is like the beautiful red roses.

Black love is like a beautiful piece of artwork.

Black love is like driving through the beautiful countryside.

Black love is like going on a long hike.

Black love is from God, who created black love to make this world a better place to live in.

God foreknew that black love would suffer long in this prejudiced world.

God foreknew that black love would be looked down on like trash in the trash dump.

God foreknew that black love would be bruised by injustice.

God foreknew that black love would be beaten up by prejudice.

God foreknew that black love would be judged by judgmental people.

God foreknew that black love would be knocked down and kicked around by discrimination.

God foreknew that black love would be terrorized by inequities.

God foreknew that black love would be ridiculed by stereotyping.

God foreknew that black love would be laughed at by those with a superiority complex.

God loves black love that knows how to worship Him.

God loves black love that knows how to obey Him.

God loves black love that knows how to hold onto Him.

God loves black love that loves His Son, Jesus Christ.

God loves black love that loves other races of people.

God loves black love to take up to heaven when his Son, Jesus Christ, comes back again.

God loves black love regardless of black love being degraded by the devil and his human agents.

Black love is like the king of the jungle.

Black love is like a beautiful rainbow.

Black love is like winning a marathon race.

Black love is like winning a gold medal.

God loves black love and has allowed black love to exist through the good days and bad days.

God loves black love regardless of the many black people who have given up on black love because of their evil deeds.

Listen to the Holy Spirit

One day, I was driving up to an intersection where the light was green.

As I drove up to the intersection, I heard the sound of a fire truck while someone else blew their car horn behind me.

A still, small voice told me not to drive through the intersection, even though I had a green light and the sound of that car horn behind me was tempting me to drive through.

A few seconds after I stopped at the green light, the fire truck went speeding past me and I was so glad that I had listened to the Holy Spirit telling me to stop.

If I hadn't listened to the Holy Spirit, I would have driven through that intersection and the fire truck would have crashed into my car.

I don't know if that driver behind me heard the fire truck, but when the Holy Spirit spoke to me so crystal clear, I listened and made the choice to do something that turned out to be a matter of life or death for me.

I am so glad that I listened to and obeyed the voice of the Holy Spirit, who was right on time to tell me to stop at that green light instead of driving on through, even though another driver behind me was in a hurry to get to wherever she wanted to go.

That driver's rush was not worth me driving through that intersection, and the Holy Spirit knew that it was not worth me risking my life.

There is Something Bigger Going On

There is something bigger going on than what is going on down in the deepest valley.

There is something bigger going on than what is going on top of the highest mountain top.

There is something bigger going on than what is going on down in the deepest ocean.

There is something bigger going on than what is going on in all the nations.

There is something bigger going on than what is going on in the jungle.

There is something bigger going on than what is going on in theories.

There is something bigger going on than what is going on in our minds.

There is something bigger going on than what is going on in our hearts.

There is something bigger going on than what is going on in science.

There is something bigger going on than what is going on in technology.

There is something bigger going on than what is going on about what the Bible says.

There's something bigger going on than what is going on in this world.

There is something bigger going on than what is going on in the universe.

There is something bigger going on and that is God, who is bigger than this world, bigger than the universe and bigger than heaven, yet God can shrink down small enough to live in our hearts.

Jesus is Freedom

Jesus is freedom because Jesus is the truth that will set us free.

No other freedom can rise above Jesus, who freed the blind to see again.

Jesus fed thousands of people and freed them from hunger.

Jesus freed many people from being possessed with demons.

Jesus freed the lame and made them walk again.

Jesus freed the sick and they got well when He lived here in this world.

Jesus is freedom that will set you and me free from living in sin.

Jesus freed many people from their unbelief when He lived here on earth without sin.

Jesus was the only one who was free from sin when He lived here on earth.

Freedom has come with a heavy price for many people.

Jesus paid a heavy price to set you and me free from the devil's bondage.

Jesus paid a heavy price to set you and me free from being doomed to go to hell.

There is no bondage in Jesus Christ, who is everlasting freedom.

Where freedom abounds, it is because of Jesus Christ, who is the origin of freedom all around the world.

Many people will put themselves in bondage by making bad choices.

Many people's bad choices put many other people in the bondage of oppression.

Jesus doesn't put anyone in bondage for loving and obeying Him.

Sin will put you and me in bondage, but Jesus is freedom.

Jesus lived among sinners to set us free from the bondage of the devil.

We Have to be Like Little Children

We have to be like little children to enter into the kingdom of God.

No matter how bad life's situations can be, little children will find the time to play with one another like nothing bad is going on around them.

They will play with one another with so much joy.

They may fight one another, but soon they will be friends again.

They hold no grudges against each other.

Many adults will quarrel with one another and hold grudges for years and years.

We can't enter into the kingdom of God with that attitude.

Children will trust that their parents will take care of them without asking their parents any questions.

Children will totally depend on their parents to provide their daily needs.

We adults don't always put our trust in the Lord to supply all of our needs.

We often depend on ourselves.

We can't enter into the kingdom of God with that attitude.

We have to be like little children and not worry about how we will survive in this world that the Lord Jesus Christ created and owns for you and me to cast our cares upon Him every day.

We have to be like little children to enter into the kingdom of God.

Little children are humble and not proud like many adults who will put their trust in themselves to solve all of their problems.

In Heaven

The grand prize in heaven came to this world to give you and me a race to run to get our prize that will be grand when we see Jesus Christ, our grand prize in heaven.

The King of heaven came to this world as a lowly baby, and you and I are spiritual babies in the presence of the King in heaven who showed us that real meaning of humility.

The Supremacy in heaven came to this world to give you and me His supreme love that brings unity in the church for everyone to be one in the body of Jesus Christ.

The Democracy in heaven came to this world to represent you and me in heaven for choosing Him to liberate our souls from the devil.

The Warrior in heaven came to this world to give you and me the victory over our battles with sin that we battle every day.

The Beauty in heaven came to this world to give you and me a beautiful, renewed life to live unto Him, our Lord Jesus Christ.

The Judge in heaven came to this world to give you and me the authority to one day judge the fallen angels when we get to heaven.

The God in heaven came to this world in His trinity godhead that John the Baptist witnessed to when he baptized Jesus Christ for you and me to be baptized and die in self and become a new creature in Jesus Christ.

The Problem is Me

The problem is me, who no one else can choose for.

The problem is me, because no one else has my motives and intentions and my mind to think for me.

The problem is me, because no one else can read my mind and know what problems I have inside of me.

Jesus Christ gave up his life to save me from my sins.

The problem is me, who no one else can be a living sermon for in my place.

The problem is me, who is a living soul who has to work out my own soul's salvation.

The problem is me, who can only have control over what I say and do because no one else can control me.

The problem is me, who the Lord allowed to be born and to live in this world where no one else can solve the problem of me.

Before I was born, the Lord knew that I would be a problem to the free will existence.

The problem is me, who must love the Lord and love my neighbors so that I can solve the problem of me.

Want to be Self-Sufficient

Many people want to be self-sufficient every day, but they don't believe that they need the Lord's help.

Many people want to rely on themselves to get things done without the help of the Lord.

Many people believe they don't need the Lord's help for anything they do.

It's the Lord who gives you and me life, health and the strength to live.

Many people believe that they can do what the Lord doesn't do for them.

Many people believe that they are so self-sufficient, until they get very sick and can't do anything for themselves.

Many people believe that they are self-sufficient until things don't go their way.

Many people believe that they are self-sufficient and can supply their own wants and needs.

They don't believe that the Lord can supply their needs and some of their wants.

Many people have regrets for depending on themselves and not depending on the Lord.

What can anybody do without the Lord giving us life, health and strength to do the things we need to do?

There is no self-sufficient man or woman, because it's the Lord who is self-sufficient and will do for you and me what we can't do for ourselves.

You and I can't do all things like the Lord, so our self-sufficiency will always fall short of the glory of God.

There are No Big Sins and Little Sins

There are no big sins and little sins, because all sin is breaking God's holy law.

Many people believe that they are only telling a little lie, but a lie is a sin and sin is sin to the Lord.

Many people believe that drinking alcohol is a little sin, but a sin is a sin to the Lord, who our bodies belong to so the Lord can dwell in us.

Some may believe that you and I committed a big sin, while they think they themselves committed a little sin.

Many people believe that the Lord will excuse the sin they believe is little, but sin is sin to the Lord.

There are no big sins and little sins to the Lord, who shows no favoritism toward anyone who sins against Him, whether they're rich or poor.

The Lord shows no favoritism toward anyone who sins against Him, whether they're educated or not educated.

The Lord shows no favoritism toward anyone who sins against Him, whether they're beautiful or not beautiful.

The Lord shows no favoritism toward anyone who sins against Him, whether they're famous or not famous.

People will believe that killing someone is a big sin, but gossiping about someone is a little sin, but a sin is a sin to the Lord.

There are no big sins and little sins to the Lord, because the wages of sin is death just like the Bible says.

Don't Compare

Don't compare yourself with other people, because God wonderfully made you In His Image.

No one else in this world is better than you, no matter how talented they are.

Don't compare yourself or think you're better than others who God wonderfully made In His image.

There is only one you and no one else can be you.

Don't compare yourself with others who are not perfect without any sin in their lives.

Making comparisons means you don't accept yourself for who you are.

Making comparisons is putting yourself down under someone else.

Making comparisons puts limits on you.

Making comparisons is putting your self-esteem down.

Making comparisons means you're not feeling good about yourself.

Making comparisons and thinking more highly of yourself and that you're better than others can be a downfall for you.

Don't compare yourself with other people who make some mistakes just like you.

Comparing yourself with someone else is of the devil, who tried to compare himself with God when he was up in heaven.

The devil's comparison caused him to be proud, which got him cast out of heaven.

Don't compare yourself with other people who can't save themselves from being lost in their sins.

Jesus Christ never compared himself with God, who He humbled Himself unto with obedience to God's will In the garden of Gethsemane.

If We Make it to Heaven

If we make it to heaven, we will be made like the angels in heaven.

If we make it to heaven, there won't be any marriages in heaven.

There won't be any making babies in heaven.

There won't be any sex in heaven.

If we make it to heaven, we won't need a soulmate in heaven.

The angels don't get married in heaven.

The angels don't have sex in heaven.

The angels don't make babies in heaven.

The angels have no soulmates in heaven.

If we make it to heaven, we will be made like the angels in heaven.

There won't be any courtship in heaven.

There won't be any dating in heaven.

There won't be romantic relationships in heaven.

The angels don't have courtship in heaven.

The angels don't date in heaven.

The angels don't have romantic relationships in heaven.

If we make it to heaven, we will be made like the angels, just like the Bible says.

God didn't create the angels to procreate, God created man and woman to procreate here on earth but not in heaven, if we make it there.

Limitation

Everybody in this world has a limitation.

One person can't do everything, and many people have more limitations than other people.

You might know how to fly a plane, but you may be limited in knowledge of how to repair a plane.

You might know how to cook, but you may be limited to own a restaurant.

You might be a judge, but you may be limited when it comes to driving a stick-shift car.

You might be a police officer, but you may be limited when cleaning your house.

You might be a politician, but you may be limited when playing a game of checkers.

You might be a soldier, but may be limited when it comes to repairing your car.

Everybody has a limitation and is not able to do everything.

You might be a doctor, but you may be limited when it comes to repairing a water leak in your roof.

You might be an engineer, but you may be limited when it comes to decorating your house.

You might be a tractor-trailer truck driver, but you may be limited when it comes to writing a book.

One person can't do everything, because God gives us different talents and skills.

On the Highway Roads

So many people will drive fast on the highway roads.

You and I can drive the speed limit, but they will speed past us.

Some people will drive right up on our bumpers before they change lanes.

There are many drivers with all kinds of vehicles speeding past you and me like we are in their way.

There is a highway road of life where many people will tailgate your faithfulness to the Lord. There is a highway road of life where many people will speed past your honesty to make you look like a liar.

There is a highway road of life where many people will get into an accident with your obedience unto the Lord and try to cause you to disobey the Lord.

So many people will speed on the highway road every day and every night.

So many people will drive up on the bumper of our peace of mind to disturb our relationship with the Lord Jesus Christ, who has a highway road that leads us to heaven.

On Jesus' highway road to heaven, no one is speeding because we will all get to heaven at the same time.

On Jesus' highway road to heaven, there are no cars driving up on anyone's bumper because there is plenty of space for everyone to be saved in Jesus Christ.

On Jesus' highway road, there will be no accidents of not being sealed in Jesus Christ, because Jesus' highway road is only for the holy and righteous to use to make it to heaven.

Opinions

A lot of people love to give their opinions and try to make them fit in with God's holy word.

A lot of people love to give their opinions with no truth to back it up.

A lot of people love to give their opinions about things they have no knowledge of.

A lot of people love to give their opinions about what they haven't experienced.

A lot of people love to give their opinions about what other people say.

A lot of people love to give their opinions about what other people do.

A lot of people love to give their opinions, even though their opinions are so far away from the truth.

A lot of people love to give their opinions with a cold heart.

A lot of people love to give their opinions with a twisted mind.

A lot of church folks love to give their opinions about what God's word means to them.

Many church folks love to add their opinions to God's holy word.

Who are Not Good

There are many people who are not good to talk to.

They will talk about things to discourage you and me.

There are people who want to be right about everything they say.

There are people who want to be right about everything they do.

What you and I say means nothing to them.

What you and I do means nothing to them.

There are some church folks who are not good when they talk about the Lord.

They will make the Lord look like a controlling God.

There are people who are not good to think about.

They will be on your mind in a bad way.

There are people who are not good to look at.

They will give you and me evil eye looks.

There are people who are not good to help.

They will try to use you and me.

There are people who are not good to be a friend to.

They will take you and me for granted.

There are people who are not good to work with.

They will want you and me to do the work that they are supposed to do.

There are people who are not good to listen to.

They will give you and me bad advice.

There are people who are not good to be around.

They will set bad examples for you and me.

There are people who are not good to go anywhere with.

They won't care about taking up a lot of your time.

It Can Take

It can take your sermons to bring someone to the Lord.

It can take your Sabbath school lessons to bring someone to the Lord.

It can take your hand to bring someone to the Lord.

It can take your friendship to bring someone to the Lord.

It can take a sickness to bring someone to the Lord.

It can take a hardship to bring someone to the Lord.

It can take your prayers to bring someone to the Lord.

It can take your kindness to bring someone to the Lord.

It can take your joy to bring someone to the Lord.

It can take our good health to bring someone to the Lord.

It can take your faith to bring someone to the Lord.

It can take your love to bring people to the Lord.

It can take your peace of mind to bring someone to the Lord.

It can take your hope to bring someone to the Lord.

It can take your honesty to bring someone to the Lord.

It can take your forgiveness to bring someone to the Lord.

It can take your patience to bring someone to the Lord.

It can take your humility to bring someone to the Lord.

It can take your love to bring someone to the Lord.

It can take your good deeds to bring someone to the Lord.

Can't Get Ahead of the Lord

You and I can't get ahead of the Lord to do something that only the Lord can do.

You and I can't get ahead of the Lord by what we say that will not come to pass if the Lord doesn't allow it to come to pass.

No one can get ahead of the Lord to truly fail.

No one can make any plans ahead of the Lord to crush our plans if we don't wait on Him.

There are people who have tried to get ahead of the Lord and suffered for it.

There are people who have tried to get ahead of the Lord and got depressed.

There are people who have tried to get ahead of the Lord and regretted it.

There are people who tried to get ahead of the Lord and lost their lives.

No one can see trouble ahead of the Lord.

No one can see pain ahead of the Lord.

No one can see misfortunes ahead of the Lord.

No one can see heartaches ahead of the Lord.

Who can get ahead of the Lord and live to tell it?

We can only stay within our bounds because we can never get ahead of the Lord Jesus Christ who was always ahead of everyone when He lived here on earth without sin.

The devil can never get ahead of the Lord with his very limited power compared to the all-powerful Lord and savior Jesus Christ, who can do anything but fail you and me.

It Will Not Always Be Easy

What you and I love to do will not always be easy to do, no matter how much we love doing it.

Just because we love doing something doesn't mean that it will be so easy to do.

There are times when we may get tired of doing what we love to do.

We can love doing something too much and want to take a break.

It will not always be easy to do what you and I love to do.

You may be good at doing great things and may experience something hard to do.

You may be good at doing encouraging things that may not always be easy for you to do and you may get discouraged.

No matter how much you love to travel, it will not always be easy to travel.

No matter how much you love to learn new things, it will not always be easy to learn new things.

No matter how much you love to fly a plane, it will not always be easy to fly a plane, especially when there is some turbulence in the atmosphere.

No matter how much you love to sing, it will not always be easy to do when your throat gets sore and make it hard to sing.

Even though you love the Lord Jesus Christ, it will not always be easy to love the Lord when your sinful nature makes it hard for you to love the Lord without ever needing to confess and repent.

Our Works Unto the Lord

We do not do our works unto the Lord to get popularity.

Our works are not to get personal advancement.

Our works unto the Lord are to build up the church.

Our works unto the Lord are to give the glory and praise to the Lord Jesus Christ.

Our works unto the Lord are to give testimonies about the Lord.

Our works unto the Lord are to let the people of the world know that we love the Lord.

Our works unto the Lord are to let the people of the world know that we believe in Jesus Christ.

Our works unto the Lord are to let the people of the world know that we live our lives unto the Lord.

Our works unto the Lord are to let the people of the world know that we obey the Lord.

Our works unto the Lord are to let the people of the world know that we are saved in Jesus Christ.

Our works unto the Lord are not to get rich.

Our works unto the Lord give us no entitlement to get God's favor above others.

Our works unto the Lord Jesus Christ are to confirm our faith in the Lord.

When We Learn New Rights

When we learn new rights, we are to live by the new rights along with the old rights.

Right is right, no matter whether it's the old rights or new rights.

Doing what is right every day will make the wrongs look so foolish.

When we learn new rights from God's holy word, we are to live by them.

We can never learn enough of the rights in this world that is corrupt with so many wrongdoings.

Learning new things that are right will surely sharpen our minds.

Learning new things that are right will surely ease our minds.

Learning new things that are right will surely make us more intelligent.

Learning new things that are right will surely make us more mature.

Learning new things that are right will surely set us free from doing a lot of wrong things.

When we learn new right things and join them to the old right things in our life, we will surely be on our way to great achievements in life.

Anyone who doesn't know God's holy word and decides to read it will learn right things that will be new right things to them.

God will never run out of new right things, because God is righteous to do everything right, whether it's old rights or new rights.

Spiritually Inactive

A lot of people are active in going to a football game.

A lot of people are active in going to a basketball game.

A lot of women are active in shopping in the malls.

A lot of people are active in traveling here and there.

A lot of people are active in going to college.

A lot of people are active in exercising.

A lot of children are active in playing video games.

A lot of people are active in politics.

A lot of people are active in going to a concert.

A lot of people are active in going to court.

A lot of people are active in doing bad things.

A lot of people are spiritually inactive in praying to the Lord.

A lot of people are spiritually inactive in going to church.

A lot of people are spiritually inactive in reading the bible.

A lot of people are spiritually inactive in working for the Lord.

A lot of people are spiritually inactive in loving their neighbors.

A lot of people are spiritually inactive in living their lives unto Jesus Christ.

Trials

There are short trials and there are long trials, and every Christ will go through some kind of trial for Jesus' name sake.

Trials are to make us strong in the Lord.

Trials are to make us spiritually mature in the Lord.

Trials are to humble us unto the Lord.

Trials are to strengthen our faith in the Lord.

The short trials can prepare us for the long trials.

The short trials can strengthen us for the long trials.

The long trials can surely build a strong relationship with the Lord for us.

The long trials can surely strengthen our prayer life.

The long trials can surely help us to keep our trust in the Lord.

The long trials can surely help us to deny ourselves and keep Jesus first in our lives.

The long trials can surely help to bring out the best in us as we hold onto the Lord.

The long trials can surely let us know how much we need the Lord.

Every true Christian will go through some kind of trial for Jesus' name sake.

The long trials can surely help us to be selfless.

The long trials can surely soften our hearts and help us to love people sincerely.

There are short trials and there are long trials that we will go through to make us pure like gold in this world of many rebellious people looking like imitation gold that has no value.

The world can't buy God's pure gold of holy saints.

It's Easy to Blame Someone Else

It's easy to blame someone else for your mistakes.

Many people won't admit the mistakes they make.

Admitting your mistakes is being honest with yourself.

Admitting your mistakes is setting yourself free from lying to yourself.

It's easy to blame someone else for your mistakes that will catch up with you even if you don't admit them.

Admitting your mistakes will surely make you very mature.

Admitting your mistakes will cause people to trust you.

Admitting your mistakes will help you to see your own flaws.

It's easy to blame someone else or your mistakes, and many people don't like to admit their mistakes.

Admitting your mistakes is moving on to growing up mentally, emotionally and spiritually.

Admitting your own mistakes and admitting my own mistakes is making peace within ourselves.

It's easy to blame someone else for your mistakes that the Lord is not pleased with.

If you and I blame someone else for our mistakes, we are sinning against God.

Will Use Other People

Many people will use other people like they're nothing more than using a toothbrush and toothpaste to brush our teeth.

Many people will use other people like they're nothing more than using a dust cloth to dust off the furniture.

Many people will use other people like they're nothing more than using a plate to put food in.

Many people will use other people like they're nothing more than a spoon and fork to eat food with.

Many people will use other people like they're nothing more than a mop used to clean the dirty floor.

Many people will use other people like they're nothing more than a candle used to light a dark room.

Many people will use other people like they're nothing more than a chair to sit down on.

Many people will use other people like they're nothing more than a TV remote to turn on the TV with.

Many people will use other people like they're nothing more than a toothpick to pick out the food between your teeth.

Many people will use other people like they're nothing more than a hat to cover your head.

Many people will use other people like they're nothing more than a table to put your plate of food on.

Many people will use other people like they're nothing more than a vacuum cleaner to vacuum their carpet.

Many people will use other people like they're nothing more than a stove to cook their food.

Many people will try to use the Lord to give them what they want.

Many people will try to use the Lord to answer their selfish prayers.

Many people will try to use the Lord to overlook their sins.

Will Act Like They Don't' Know You

Some people will act like they don't know you when they move into a new house.

Some people will act like they don't know you when they get a new car or truck.

Some people will act like they don't know you when they get their college degree.

Some people will act like they don't know you when they get a high-paying job.

Some people will act like they don't' know you when they move up in life.

Some people will act like they don't know you if they get rich.

God hates a proud look that causes many people to head towards a fall.

Being proud is of the devil who became proud up in heaven because he was the most beautiful angel who God created.

Some people will act like they don't know you if they become famous.

Some people will act like they don't' know you when they join the military.

Some people will act like they don't know you and me if we get so sick that we can't do anything.

If the Lord Isn't in It

I will not be blessed by what you say and you will not be blessed by what I say if the Lord isn't in it.

I will not be blessed by what you do and you will not be blessed by what I do if the Lord isn't in it.

I will not be blessed by your ministry and you will not be blessed by my ministry if the Lord isn't in it.

If the Lord isn't in what we say, it is so vain.

If the Lord is not in what we do, it is so vain.

The Lord is not in selfish ambitions.

The Lord is not in self-sufficiency.

The Lord is not in selfish pride.

I will not be blessed by your life and you will not be blessed by my life if the Lord isn't in our lives.

I will not be blessed by your dream and you will not be blessed by my dream if the Lord isn't in our dreams.

The Mystery of God

The mystery of God is in His holy word, where God reveals his mysteries to you and me.

There are many unsolved mysteries in this world where many mysteries will never be solved.

Many people are missing and where they've gone is a mystery.

We can pack up something that has great value to us and then not be able to find it and it becomes a mystery to us as to where it went.

It's like a mystery that God created Lucifer and knew that Lucifer would rebel against Him.

It's like a mystery that Adam and Eve were warned by God not to eat the fruit from the tree of good knowledge and evil.

It's like a mystery that they disobeyed God after He had warned them.

Many people don't know the mystery of God because they don't study His holy word.

Many people will search for the mysteries in the universe, only to find out what they haven't seen in the universe.

The greatest mystery is found in God's holy word.

God's holy word reveals all mysteries in this world from the beginning of time, and these mysteries stun sinful men.

It was like a mystery when God put a mark on Cain to let other men know not to kill him because he had killed his brother Abel.

Enough of Right

Many people know enough of right and don't do all the right that they know.

Many people know enough of right not to kill.

Many people know enough of right not to steal.

Many people know enough of right not to lie.

A criminal knows enough of right that they know what they do is wrong and will run away from the police.

A criminal knows that it's not right to kill.

A criminal knows that it's not right to steal.

Many people know enough of right to treat people right.

Many little children don't know enough of right, so their parents must teach them what is right.

God gives us enough of right in His holy word for us to live right by day after day.

A criminal knows enough of right to keep the law.

Many criminals know enough of right that they know what they do is wrong so they hide away from the police.

Many people know enough of right to know that it's right to talk right.

Many people know enough of right to know that it's right to act right.

Many people know enough of right to know that God is always right when everyone else is wrong.

Politics are About

Politics are about what can he do and what can she do.

Politics are about what has he done and what has she done.

Politics are about "what can you do for me?"

Politics are about "what have you done for me?"

Politics are about "I can do this" and "I can do that."

Politics are about "I can do what you can't do."

Politics are about "I have done what you haven't done."

Politics are about "I am smarter than you."

Politics are about "I am greater than you."

Politics are about "I can get more things done than you."

Politics are about "I can get the job done better than you."

There shouldn't' be any politics in the church, because everyone is supposed to be in unity for the same purpose — to build up the church.

There shouldn't' be any quarreling among church folds to see who is the greatest in the church.

Politics are about dividing people.

Politics are about "what I can do for you."

Politics are about "I will change this" and "I will change that."

Politics are about "I can do what has never been done before."

Jesus Christ, our Lord, was up against politics when He live on earth without sin.

Even Jesus' disciples wanted Jesus to rule over the government.

Is our life like...

Is our life like the sun that shines?

Is our life like the moon that glows?

Is our life like the stars that sparkle?

Is our life like the wind that blows here and there?

Is our life like the seasons that change?

Is our life like a high mountain?

Is our life like the deep oceans?

Is our life like a heatwave?

Is our life like a snow blizzard?

Is our life like a forest fire?

Is our life like the rain that falls?

Is our life like the river that flows?

Is our life like a rooftop that leaks?

Is our life like a brand-new car?

Is our life like a treasure chest?

Is our life like the open wide sky?

Is our life like a secret closet?

Is our life like a highway road?

Is our life like a country road?

Is our life like a cruise ship?

Is our life like a deep mystery?

Is our life like a rocket launching?

Is our life like broken glass?

Is our life like a lighthouse?

Is our life like an open book?

Is our life like a war?

Is our life like heaven?

Is our life like Jesus Christ?

When I See You, O Lord

When I see you, O Lord, You will wipe away all of my tears.

When I see you, O Lord, You will give me unspeakable joy.

When I see you, my Lord Jesus Christ, you will make me so happy.

When I see you, O Lord, You will give me immeasurable strength.

When I see you, O Lord, You will build me up like a high tower.

When I see you, my Lord Jesus Christ, You will make my life complete forever and ever.

When I see you, O Lord, You will give me treasures of peace.

When I see you, O Lord, You will fill my life with eternal youth.

When I see you, O Lord, You will take me to heaven.

When I see you, my Lord Jesus Christ, You will give me the wonders of Your everlasting love.

When I see you, O Lord, You will give me Your eternal glory.

When I see you, my Lord Jesus Christ, You will make me eternal.

When I see you, O Lord, You will make my destiny perfect.

When I see you, my Lord Jesus Christ, You will set me eternally free.

When I see you, O Lord, You will teach me eternal things.

When I see you, O Lord, I will know that You saved me from my sins.

It Doesn't Matter

It doesn't matter who you are.

It's always good to put the Lord first and above you.

It doesn't matter where you live.

It's always good to live your life unto the Lord.

It doesn't matter what you say.

It's always good to believe what the Lord says.

It doesn't matter what you do.

It's always good to do the Lord's will.

It doesn't matter where you go.

It's always good to go where the Lord tells you to go.

It doesn't matter how rich you are.

It's always good to give your tithes and offerings to the Lord.

It doesn't matter how poor you are.

It's always good to give what little you have to the Lord.

It doesn't matter how much you know.

It's always good to know the Lord.

It doesn't matter how great you are.

It's always good to exalt the Lord, who is greater than you.

It doesn't matter how much you win.

It's always good to humble yourself unto the Lord, who is always victorious.

It doesn't matter how many mistakes you make.

It's always good to trust the Lord, who is perfect without sin.

It doesn't matter how good you are.

It's always good to confess and repent unto the Lord, whose goodness leads to repentance.

The Lord Owns Everything

The Lord owns everything in this world.

The Lord owns everybody in this world, where you and I don't own anything because everything will burn up in hell one day.

A man doesn't own his wife.

A woman doesn't own her husband.

Parents don't own their children.

A man doesn't own his girlfriend.

A woman doesn't own her boyfriend.

Rich people don't own their wealth.

A man doesn't own his body.

A woman doesn't own her body.

No one owns their body.

The Lord owns our bodies.

The Lord owns our breath.

The Lord owns everything.

The Lord owns this world.

The Lord owns the universe.

The Lord owns the heavens.

The Lord owns hell.

There is nothing that the Lord doesn't own.

There is no one who the Lord doesn't own.

The Lord owns all the angels in heaven.

The Lord owns all the fallen angels.

The Lord owns all the other worlds.

The Lord owns all seen things. The Lord owns all unseen things.

You and I can't call anything our own.

The Lord owns the living.

The Lord owns the dead.

The Lord owns the grave.

You and I don't own anything that won't be any use to us in the grave.

Everything that we have is a loan from the Lord.

Sin as always on the attack

Sin is always on the attack, coming after us with its lust to bite us and chew us up.

Sin is always on the attack, coming after us with its pride to bite us and chew us up.

Sin is always on the attack, coming after us with its greed to bite us and chew us up.

Sin as always on the attack, coming after us with its lies to bite us and chew us up.

Sin as always on the attack, coming after us with its selfishness to bite us and chew us up.

Sin can attack but can't bite us and chew us up if we stay in prayer unto the Lord.

Sin can attack us but can't bite us and chew us up if we keep our faith in the Lord.

Sin can attack us but can't bite us and chew us up if we love and obey the Lord.

Sin is always on the attack, coming after us with its pretense to bite us and chew us up.

Sin is always on the attack, coming after us with its rebellion to bite us and chew us up.

Sin can attack us but can't bite us and chew us up if we are saved in Jesus Christ, our Lord and Savior.

Mental Powers

Intelligence is a mental power that you may have.

Genius is a mental power that you may have.

Brilliance is a mental power that you may have.

Wisdom is a mental power that you may have.

Knowledge is a mental power that you may have.

Encouragement is a mental power that you may have.

Motivation is a mental power that you may have.

Knowing a lot of right is a mental power that you may have.

Knowing a lot of wrong is a mental power that you may have.

Knowing a lot of good is a mental power that you may have.

Knowing a lot of evil is a mental power that you may have.

Mental powers are from the Lord, who gives us mental powers for His glory.

Everyone has some kind of mental power, but everyone doesn't know how to use their mental power to survive in this world.

Even a baby has a built-in mental power to cry and let you know that something is wrong with him or her.

Mental powers are used to serve the Lord, which our physical body will do under the command of our mental powers.

I Can't Rely On

I can't rely on my own strength, because it can't keep me strong like Your strength, O Lord.

I can't rely on my own eyes, because they can't see all that You see, O Lord.

I can't rely on my own ears, because they can't hear all that You hear, O Lord.

I can't rely on my own hands, because they can't hold all existence like You can, O Lord.

I can't rely on my own feet, because I can't walk everywhere that You can walk to, O Lord.

I can't rely on my own legs, because I can't stand on all the stars like you can stand on all the stars, O Lord.

I can't rely on me, who can't save me like You can do, O Lord

I can't rely on my own life, because I can't live without you, O Lord, giving me breath in my body.

I can't rely on anyone, because no one can do all the things that You can do, O Lord.

I can't rely on my own arms, because they can't wrap around the universe like Your arms can, O Lord.

The Righteous and Wicked

The Lord is good to the righteous and wicked.

The Lord sends down the rain on the righteous and wicked.

The Lord shines down the sunlight on the righteous and wicked.

The Lord provides food for the righteous and wicked.

The Lord supplies the needs of the righteous and wicked.

The Lord shows mercy to the righteous and wicked.

The Lord gives His grace to the righteous and wicked.

The Lord gives his love to the righteous and wicked.

The difference between the righteous and wicked is that the righteous love the Lord, and the wicked don't love the Lord.

The difference between the righteous and the wicked is the righteous are saved in Jesus Christ, and the wicked are lost in their sins.

The difference between the righteous and the wicked is that the righteous are the church of Jesus Christ, and the wicked are the human agents of the devil.

The difference between the righteous and the wicked is that the righteous will go to heaven one day and the wicked will go to hell one day.

We Just Don't Always Know

We just don't always know how the devil will try to tempt us to sin against God.

We just don't always know when the devil will try to tempt us to sin against God.

We just don't always know who the devil will try to use to tempt us to sin against God.

We just don't always know where the devil will try to tempt us to sin against God.

We can be in our homes, and the devil will try to tempt us to sin against God.

We can be in a store, and the devil will try to tempt us to sin against God.

We can be on the job, and the devil will try to tempt us to sin against God.

We just don't always know what the devil will use to try to tempt us into sinning against God.

We just don't always know ourselves who the devil will try to use to sin against God.

We can be right in the church, and the devil will try to tempt us to sin against God.

Our only safe place is staying in prayer, which gets our minds on God and away from sinning against God.

We just don't always know why God allows the devil to try to tempt us when we are weak.

Our weakness can't overtake us, because Jesus Christ got the victory over our sins so that we can resist the devil and make him flee from us in our weaknesses.

In Danger

Many people will put their lives in danger like it's a sport to play.

Many people will put their lives in danger like there's nothing to it.

Many people will put their lives in danger like it's no big deal.

Many people will put their lives in danger and will joke about it.

Many people will put their lives in danger and laugh about it.

Many people will put their lives in danger and think nothing of it.

Many people will put their lives in danger and won't walk away from it.

Many people will put their lives in danger and won't run away from it.

Many people will put their lives in danger and believe that they are not in danger.

Many people will put their lives in danger and will boast about it.

Danger doesn't care about how brave you are.

Danger doesn't care about who you are.

Danger doesn't care about how rich you are.

Danger doesn't care about how poor you are.

Danger doesn't care about how educated you are.

Danger doesn't care about how strong you are.

Danger doesn't care about how beautiful you are.

Danger will take you and me to the grave if the Lord allows it.

The Lord will never tell us to do anything dangerous that would cause our souls to be lost.

When it's Our Time
to go to the Grave

When it's our time to go to the grave, there is nothing we can do about it.

When it's our time to go to the grave, no doctor can do anything about it.

When it's our time to go to the grave, no one can do anything about it.

When it's our time to go to the grave, no prayers can do anything about it.

When the Lord calls us to the Land of the Dead, that is where we will go with no interruptions.

When the Lord calls us to the Land of the Dead, we can't talk our way out of it.

When the Lord calls us to the Land of the Dead, we can't work our way out of it.

When the Lord calls us to the Land of the Dead, we can't buy our way out of it.

When it's our time to go to the grave, no one can stop it.

Many doctors have tried to stop the Lord God from taking many of their sick patients to the Land of the Dead.

They didn't succeed, because God has the final call.

We don't know when it will be our time to go to the grave, but our lives should be all about loving and obeying the Lord Jesus Christ.

When our life is over in this world, we will live again when Jesus Christ comes back to take us to Heaven if we died being saved in Him.

Don't Lay Up Your Treasures in this World

Don't lay up your treasures in this world where earthquakes can destroy them.

Don't lay up your treasures in this world where wildfires can destroy them.

Don't lay up your treasures in this world where floods can destroy you.

Don't lay up your treasures in this world where mudslides can destroy them.

Don't lay up your treasures in this world where tornadoes can destroy them.

Don't lay up your treasures in this world where bombs can destroy them.

Don't lay up your treasures in this world where hurricanes and destroy them.

Don't lay up your treasures in this world where volcano eruptions can destroy them.

Don't lay up your treasures in this world where tsunamis can destroy them.

Don't lay up your treasures in this world where evil people can destroy them.

Don't lay up your treasures in this world where sinkholes can destroy them.

Don't lay up your treasures in this world where rust can destroy them.

Don't lay up your treasures in this world where erosion can destroy them.

Don't lay up your treasures in this world where deterioration can destroy them.

Don't lay up your treasures in this world where time can destroy them.

Lay up your treasures in Heaven, where nothing can destroy them.

Lay up your treasures in Heaven, where they will always be secured by God.

Doing Their Own Will

Many people are so comfortable doing their own will.

Encouraging many people to do God's holy will causes them to feel uncomfortable, but doing God's holy will should make everyone feel so comfortable to do.

Many people are very comfortable doing their own will and speaking their own words, even though they're not in line with God's holy word.

There are so-called Christians who are not comfortable about doing everything that the Lord tells them to do in His holy word.

They will make excuses to not do everything the Lord says.

Doing the Lord's will is comfort to our souls to be saved in the Lord Jesus Christ, whose will and God's will is the same yesterday, today and forever more.

Many people are very comfortable doing their own will, and that will surely cause them to be lost in their sins.

Not Interested.

Many people are not interested in religious things.

Many people are not interested in hearing a sermon, because that is foolishness to many people who are living in their sins.

Many people are not interested in reading the Bible.

Many church folks don't read their Bible day after day.

Many people are not interested in going to church because they believe it is wasting their time to go.

Many people are not interested in their soul's salvation, and they couldn't care less about going to hell.

Many people are not interested in hearing anything about Jesus Christ.

Many people are not interested in praying to the Lord, who they believe has no power to answer their prayers.

Many people are not interested in God's Commandments because they believe that they don't have to keep them.

Many people are not interested in being a Christian.

They believe that every Christian is a hypocrite.

Many people are not interested in wanting to know God.

They believe that there is no God to get to know.

We Must Stay in Our Lane

We must stay in our lane.

We must stay out of other people's business.

We must stay in our lane.

We must not co-sign our names on someone else's loan.

We must stay in our lane.

We must not assume anything without all the facts.

We must stay in our lane.

We must not go where we are not invited.

We must stay in our lane.

We must not go where we don't belong.

We must stay in our lane.

We must not obey any law that is not in line with God's holy word.

We must stay in our lane.

We must not give money to someone who will waste it.

We must stay in our lane.

We Christians must not hang around fools.

We must stay in our lane.

We Christians must not hang around immoral people.

We must stay in our lane.

We Christians must not say one thing and then do another.

Trouble

There are people who are nothing but trouble, and it doesn't matter what color their skin is.

There are people who are trouble on the highway roads.

They will tailgate you and me.

There are people who are trouble in their own homes.

They are abusive to their spouse and children.

There are people who are trouble on their job.

They talk mean to their co-workers and overwork their employees.

There are people who are trouble in the government.

They make some laws to oppress people.

There are people who are trouble in their neighborhoods.

They disrespect their neighbors by playing loud music and parking their cars in their neighbor's parking spaces.

There are people who are trouble in their schools.

They will bully other students and fight them.

There are people who are trouble in the church.

They will try to control their brothers and sisters and make them do what they want to do.

There are people who are trouble to themselves.

They do bad things to their own bodies and cause their health to go bad.

There are People Who Will

There are people who will do you wrong and then joke about it.

There are people who will bring you down emotionally, physically, financially and spiritually if you let them bring you down.

There are people who will encourage you to do the right thing.

There are people who will use you until you put your foot down and say no.

There are people who will be nice to you to your face and talk bad about you behind your back.

There are people who will give you their last dollar to help you.

There are people who will ruin your good name if you don't give them what they want.

There are people who will kill you and be happy that you are dead.

There are people who won't leave you alone until they get what they want from you.

There are people who will lie to you and believe that what they say about you is true.

There are Christian people who will pray for you.

There are Christian people who will show you who Jesus Christ is through their actions beyond their words.

There are Christian people who truly love you and want you to be saved in Jesus Christ.

There are Christian people who won't question you about your past lifestyle after you have given your life to the Lord.

To Make Things for Our Bad

The devil loves to make things for our bad.

The Lord always knows how to make something good out of something bad.

You and I can go through some bad things that may seem to never end, but the Lord can mean it for our good to make us strong in doing His holy will.

The devil loves to make things for our bad.

No matter what bad things we go through, the Lord is for us if we keep our faith in Him who can bring that bad thing to an end.

When we are going through something bad, we don't think about what good things could come out of it.

The Lord is always on top of everything and will make a way for you and me to have some joy and peace while we go through something bad in our lives.

The devil loves to make things for our bad.

The Lord has the final word and can change our bad situations into something good to blow our minds.

The devil will always mean things for our bad, when the Lord will always mean the bad things for our good to be a blessing coming our way in time.

People Pay Attention to What You Do

People pay attention to what you do more than what you say.

Words can usually fool people, but what you do can tell the true story.

People pay attention to what you do, and that will very often get their attention more than what you say.

What you and I do is real proof of who we are.

You can say something and then change what you say, but when you do something, whether it's good or bad, it will remain the same.

People pay attention to what you do more than what you say.

You can say one thing and do another thing, but when you do something people will see it, no matter what you say.

What you do is real evidence of who you are, more than what you say.

People pay attention to what you do, even when your words can go in one ear and out the other.

When Jesus Christ lived on earth, people paid attention to what He did more than what He said to them.

Jesus always knew that He was closely watched, so Jesus always did the right thing for everyone to see.

It's always good to be nice

No matter what you go through in your life, it's always good to be nice to other people.

You may be going through something bad, but that should not stop you from being nice to other people.

You might be feeling bad, but you just don't know how someone else is feeling and they may feel much worse than you.

You just don't know what someone else has been through in their life, and that person may truly need you to be nice to him or her.

Being nice to people can truly lift them up if they are feeling down.

Being nice to people can truly give them a better outlook on life.

It's always good to be nice to people, no matter how young or old they are.

Being nice to people will help you feel better about yourself.

Being nice to a mean person can help that mean person want to change for the better.

Being nice is of the Lord, but being mean is of the devil.

The Lord is nice to everyone, even when we sin against Him and reap what we sow.

Will Try to Test Your Intelligence

Some people will try to test your intelligence to see if you know what they know.

There are people who don't want you to be smarter than them.

Some people want to know it all and don't want you to know anything.

Some people will try to test your intelligence to see if you know what they are talking about.

If you know something that some people don't know, they won't like you and will take you the wrong way if you say something they didn't think to say.

Some people will try to test your intelligence because they want to know it all and they'll try to make you look ignorant.

There are people who will test your intelligence in a good way to bring out the best in you.

There are people who will test your intelligence in a good way to esteem you.

Some people will try to test your intelligence and look down on you if you don't know what they know.

There were people who tried to test Jesus' intelligence to see if He knew what they didn't know.

They were surprised because Jesus knew all things when He lived here on earth.

There were people like the Pharisees who tried to test Jesus' intelligence to see if He would say something they would disagree with.

Every word Jesus said to them was the truth, but their intelligence was mired in sin and they did not believe Him.

What Profit a Man or Woman?

What profit a man or woman to gain college degrees and lose their soul?

What profit a man or woman to gain achievements and lose their soul?

What profit a man or woman to gain success and lose their soul?

What profit a man or woman to gain trophies and lose their soul?

What profit a man or woman to gain awards and lose their soul?

What profit a man or woman to gain wealth and lose their soul?

What profit a man or woman to gain skills and lose their soul?

What profit a man or woman to gain scholarship and lose their soul?

What profit a man or woman to gain the whole world and lose their soul?

Your soul has more worth to God than anything in this world.

There's nothing wrong with gaining things, but it is wrong to put those things above God, who gives the increases in our lives if it is in His holy will.

God will allow many wicked people to get wealth and lose it, to show that their wealth goes back to God to give to the poor.

What profit a man or woman to gain popularity and lose their soul?

What profit a man or woman to gain pleasure and lose their soul?

What profit a man or women to gain pride and lose their soul?

What profit a man or woman to gain greed and lose their soul?

What profit a man or woman to gain selfishness and lose their soul?

What profit a man or woman to gain special favors and lose their soul?

What profit a man or women to gain superiority in lose their soul?

What profit a man or woman to gain attention and lose their soul?

What profit a man or woman to gain fame and lose their soul?

What profit a man or woman to gain prestige and lose their soul?

It's not a sin to gain good things, but it is a sin to put those things above God.

There is no profit in putting anything above God.

What profit a man or woman to gain theories and lose their soul?

What profit a man or woman to gain brilliance and lose their soul?

Jesus Christ gave up His life to save you and me from our sins, not for what we can profit or gain.

Today is Our Appointed Time

Today is our appointed time to be here to choose to believe in Jesus Christ or not believe in Jesus Christ.

Today is our appointed time to exist in this world where it wasn't meant for you and me to exist in the beginning of time here on earth.

It wasn't meant for us to be born back in the bible days.

It wasn't meant for us to be born in the fifteenth century.

It wasn't meant for us to be born in the eighteenth century.

Today is our appointed time to be here to choose to love and obey Jesus Christ or choose to love and obey the devil.

We can't go back in time like some movies and TV shows portray to captivate a lot of people.

Today is our appointed time to exist and give Jesus our time, talent and tithes.

Today is our appointed time to exist and give Jesus our love and obedience unto Him.

We only get one appointed time here on earth, where all who once lived got their appointed times that Jesus gave to them.

An appointed time can be very short-lived or long-lived, according to God's holy will.

We all have an appointed time to die, and we can't question Jesus about it because Jesus always knows what's best for you and me.

Today is our appointed time to be here in the land of the living.

Everyone has an appointed time, and even a baby's time can be cut short for the baby to be destined to go to heaven when Jesus comes back again.

Everyone who ever lived had their appointed time, whether they knew right from wrong or not.

The Lord winks his eye at ignorance, and that won't keep anyone from suffering hardships for sinning against God.

Today is our appointed time to exist and give Jesus all of our hearts.

Time is short to Jesus, who is eternal.

Time is shorter than the blink of an eye to God.

Our appointed time is like one second passing by to God, who gave His Son, Jesus Christ, His appointed time here on earth to save us from our sins.

Today is our appointed time to be here, and if the Lord Jesus extends your time and my time to live a long life, the devil can't interfere, even if you and I made a lot of bad choices.

God's grace elevates our appointed time to position our souls to be saved in Jesus Christ.

Believing in God

Believing in God, who we don't see, is like breathing in and out the air that we don't see but know is there.

Believing in God, who we don't see, is like talking to someone on the phone and even though we don't see them we know they're there.

Believing in God, who we don't see, is like hearing something that we don't see but know is there.

Believing in God, who we don't see, is like swallowing food down in our stomachs that we don't see but we know we have a stomach.

Believing in God, who we don't see, is like feeling some pain that we can't see but we know the pain is there.

Believing in God, who we don't see, is like filling a tire up with air that we don't see but we know the tire can roll on the ground.

Believing in God, who we don't see, is like speaking words that we don't see but know that we have a mouth to talk.

Believing in God, who we don't see, is like the wind that we don't see but we can feel it.

Believing in God, who we don't see, is like thoughts in our minds that we don't see but we know we can bring our thoughts and words to action.

Believing in God, who we don't see, is like being blind and not seeing where to go but believing that there is somewhere to go to.

Believing in God, who we don't see, is like not seeing the sunlight on a cloudy day but knowing the sun is still there behind the clouds.

To Drive the Demons Away

There is power in having faith in Jesus to drive the demons away from you and me.

There is power in loving Jesus to drive the demons away from you and me.

There is power in obeying Jesus to drive the demons away from you and me.

There is power in being a witness of Jesus to drive the demons away from you and me.

There is power in praying to Jesus to drive the demons away from you and me.

There is power in giving testimonies about what Jesus brought us through to drive the demons away from you and me.

There is power in what Jesus is doing for us today to drive the demons away from you and me.

There is power in knowing God's holy word about Jesus to drive the demons away from you and me.

When the demons hear Jesus' name, they will tremble and flee away from you and me.

To drive the demons away is to call on Jesus' name.

To drive the demons away is to pray to Jesus every day.

To drive the demons away is to read the Bible and uplift Jesus' holy name.

There is power in Jesus' health message to drive the demons away from you and me.

There is power in our renewed life in Jesus Christ to drive the demons away from you and me.

When the demons try to tempt us to sin against God, we can pray to Jesus and trust Him to drive the demons away from you and me.

There is power in our ministry work unto Jesus to drive the demons away from you and me.

There is power in our confession and repentance unto Jesus to drive the demons away from you and me.

There is power in glorifying and praising Jesus' name to drive away the demons from you and me.

There is power in keeping our minds on Jesus to drive away the demons from you and me.

There is power in Jesus' name to drive the demons away from anyone who Jesus got the victory for when He rose from the grave with all power and authority over this sinful world to drive the demons away from you and me.

There is power in spreading the gospel of Jesus Christ to drive the demons away from you and me.

When the demons come back to us and try to tempt us to sin against God, we can ask Jesus to give us the strength to resist the devil and his demons' temptations that Jesus won't allow because He makes us strong so we can resist.

We all have the free will to choose to do God's will that is forever more powerful and stronger than the devil and his demons' temptations that can't overpower our free will to choose to love Jesus and keep His Commandments to drive the demons away from you and me.

You Can Talk to Jesus About Everything

You can talk to Jesus about everything, because he will always understand you completely.

You can't talk to your spouse about everything, because your spouse can misunderstand you and take your words the wrong way.

You can't talk to your friends about everything, because your friends can misunderstand you and take your words the wrong way.

You can't talk to your children about everything, because your children can misunderstand you and take your words the wrong way.

You can't talk to anybody about everything, because anyone can misunderstand you and take your words the wrong way.

You can talk to Jesus about everything, because He knows all of your heart, even the parts that you don't know.

You can talk to Jesus about everything, because Jesus will always understand every word you say.

You can talk to Jesus about everything, because Jesus will always understand why you feel the way you feel.

If you talk to people about everything that's on your mind, people can criticize you, but Jesus will always give you peace of mind if you trust Him and tell Him everything.

You can talk to Jesus about everything, because Jesus will always give you the right answers to all of your problems.

You can talk to Jesus about everything, because Jesus is all-wise and all-knowing and will ease your mind and heal your heart.

You can talk to Jesus about everything, because He will always judge you rightly and fairly, beyond the rights and wrongs you've done in your life.

Someone Said that God Uses the Devil

Someone said that God uses the devil, who is evil all the time.

Why would God want to use the devil for anything, when God is good all the time?

God allows the devil to tempt us, but God doesn't use the devil to tempt us.

God can't use the devil for anything that's good, because the devil can only appear to do good things but there are always evil reasons behind them.

There is nothing good about the devil for God to use, but God uses His holy angels and can use you and me to do good things.

The devil can't do anything good without an evil motive behind it.

There is nothing good in doing evil, which is what the devil loves to do and he will try to put God into his evil deeds.

Someone said that God uses the devil, but God will never let the devil use Him because He is a holy and righteous God who hates evil.

There is nothing evil about God, but the devil and his fallen angels and his human agents will try to make God look evil.

God doesn't use the devil to serve His holy purpose for you and me, but the devil's purpose is to cause our souls to be lost in hell where he will go one day.

What Good is There for Me Going to Church

What good is there for me going to church, if the Lord didn't give me a ministry to minister to my spiritual brothers and sisters in the church?

What good is there for me going to church, if I don't try my best to love all of my spiritual brothers and sisters in the church?

What good is there for me going to church if I don't deny myself and pick up my cross and follow Jesus?

What good is there for me going to church if I don't confess and repent of my sins as if I have no sins?

What good is there for me going to church if I don't want to give any testimonies about what the Lord brought me through?

What good is there for me going to church if I don't want to change my selfish ways?

What good is there for me going to church if I love to cause division in the church?

What good is there for me going to church if I love to show favoritism to certain people in the church?

What good is there for me going to church if I don't want to forgive those who offended me?

What good is there for me going to church if I don't want to love and obey the Lord Jesus Christ?

13904039R00086